My Footprint for God

What others are saying about *My Footprint for God*

I am so pleased that Kenn Edwards has written this book. It is captivating reading with much knowledge and experience shared in a compelling way. Kenn is a person that needs to be listened to as he challenges us to think and plan for the use of the financial resources God has entrusted to us. Kenn is extraordinarily well qualified to speak on this topic, and I recommend this book with great enthusiasm.

Ron Blue
Founding Director, Kingdom Advisors

In *My Footprint for God*, Kenn Edwards does a masterful job of intertwining the financial and spiritual connection we leave for future generations. One of the most profound, yet often overlooked, aspects of our Christian faith is: "Your relationship to money always impacts your relationship to God." I wish Kenn had written this book thirty years ago when I was developing my theology of money and possessions. *My Footprint for God* will have a lasting impact on anyone who seeks a God-centered view of money and desires to leave a powerful legacy for future generations.

David Briggs, Stewardship Pastor,
Central Christian Church of Arizona

In *My Footprint for God*, Kenn Edwards has done an outstanding job of integrating biblical truth and practical financial issues we all face. This very helpful and clearly written book will provide you with a roadmap to extend your influence for Christ for many years.

Howard Dayton, Founder & CEO,
Compass-Finances God's Way

My Footprint For God reflects on a crucial need for our present age: personalizing our stewardship in worship of our master. Kenn Edwards communicates the inter-relationship of spiritual legacy planning along biblical stewardship and excellent estate design. His work cuts across denominational lines and is important for everyone in your life. Bravo on one of the most needed and timely written works of this new decade.

Scott Preissler, Ph.D., Giving & Stewardship,
Georgia Baptist Mission Board

A timely message for the church today. Our spiritual legacy matters! Kenn lays out the steps for greater impact from God's blessings with a fresh look at biblical stewardship. It is amazing how so many Christians miss the importance of legacy planning as part of stewardship. His challenge on estate planning should make us take action today.

Jerry Wear, President The Great Commission
Foundation of Campus Crusade for Christ

Great content. *My Footprint for God*, symbolizing the impact of my life, is enlightening. We need to embrace this holistic stewardship message as God's stewards. The personal stories will resonate with anyone interested in their legacy. Kenn has crafted a biblical message with compassion and conviction that will impact our children and future generations for Christ. Everyone in your family needs to apply these legacy-planning principles. Our goal should be to continue our kingdom impact long after we are with the Lord. Kenn shows us how.

Joseph Padilla, Vice President for
Development and Ministry Services,
The Orchard Foundation

Spot on. A stewardship message that every Christian needs know. Kenn gives practical examples of how God uses ordinary people to accomplish His will. Much is said about leaving a legacy, but stewardship helps you build a legacy worth leaving. With the principles in *My Footprint for God*, your legacy will live on and your impact for Christ will continue. The estate planning section is a must read and a call for action for every believer.

Ray Lyne, President of Lifestyle Giving

My Footprint for God

Kenn Edwards

Copyright © Kenn Edwards 2016, 2019

ISBN 978-0-578-60006-2

Cover Art and Interior Design by kae Creative Solutions

Published in the United States of America.

Previously published by Bold Vision Books, Friendswood, TX
All rights reserved. No part of this publication may be reproduced, stored in a retrieval system, or transmitted in any form or by any means -- electronic, mechanical, photocopy, recording, or any other -- except for brief quotations in printed reviews, without the prior permission of the publisher.

Unless otherwise stated, Scripture quotations are taken from the Holy Bible, New International Version®, NIV®. Copyright © 1973, 1978, 1984, 2011 by Biblica, Inc.™ Used by permission of Zondervan. All rights reserved worldwide. The "NIV" and "New International Version" are trademarks registered in the United States Patent and Trademark Office by Biblica, Inc.™

Dedication

To my great grandmother Harriett Edwards.

Grandma Hattie's legacy
is still impacting our family today.

No time to read?

Keep up with your group by listening to the audiobook!

One-in-five Americans now listen to audiobooks according to Pew Research.

 J.D. Wininger

★★★★★ **Forces You to Ask the Right Questions of Yourself...**
Reviewed in the United States on April 2, 2019

Download your copy today:

Table of Contents

Acknowledgments	11
Introduction	13
Chapter One–More Than Money	15
Chapter Two–She Shaped My Life	25
Chapter Three–Deeper	33
Chapter Four–It's Not Mine	42
Chapter Five–Blessed to Be a Blessing	50
Chapter Six–Giving and Stewardship	58
Chapter Seven–Missed Opportunity	66
Chapter Eight–Ordinary People	74
Chapter Nine–Finding God's Plan for My Estate	82
Chapter Ten–Every Footstep Counts	90
About the Author	99
How to Host a *My Footprint for God* Conference	101
Building My Footprint for God Small Group Study Guide	103
Endnotes	105

Acknowledgments

It is nearly impossible to thank all the people who have influenced my life and ministry. The legacy of many pastors, Christian leaders, friends, family and many more. Through the years I have sat under the influence of some very good pastors who believed in me and invested in my walk with God. People like Tony Scott, who allowed me to preach my first sermon, Mike Chapman who entrusted me as an Elder and leader over my first Covenant Discipleship Group, then Michael Cook who encouraged me to develop this book and curriculum.

Many Christians have sowed into my spiritual life too. I am thankful for Jim Eubank, who shared Christ with me, Frank Hoyt who took me on my first mission trip, and several from the Gideon headquarters staff who allowed me to grow so God could use me in new and greater ways.

I'm very thankful for my parents. They taught me the value of hard work. I'll always remember the weekly prayer meetings held at our house—especially the ones held in our hayloft.

I'm indebted to my wonderful wife and our beautiful children who loved me through it all. God's faithfulness is evident in our family.

My hope is my life has impacted people along the way too. Each of us is building our footprint for God, and I pray my influence will lead many to cry out to Jesus as their personal Savior and Lord.

Introduction

As a layperson in the local church, my goal is to reach out to Christians. We have enormous potential to influence our family and our world for Christ. But, because of the routine of everyday life, it is easy to develop blind spots about our influence and legacy. Your spiritual life matters!

This book is designed to be a common-sense approach to the importance of our legacy. Every decision I make today has an impact on eternity. The depth of my walk with God, the way I handle money, and my priorities in life will influence my children and those around me for Christ—or not.

Our world needs men and women who live the abundant life for all to see.

Chapter One

More than Money

It was a Mother's Day I'll never forget. Mom's health had been failing for some time, and now she lived in a special residential home. Living 2,000 miles from her, we did not get to see each other as often as we would have liked. Each visit became special because we did not know if this would be our last. Her caregiver had gone the extra mile and prepared a private Mother's Day lunch for the two of us to enjoy.

During the previous six months, mom had experienced several mini-strokes. On good days she could put together a few words in short sentences, but she easily became confused. This confusion made communication almost impossible. That Mother's Day was no exception.

A card table had been set-up in mom's room for our private Mother's Day lunch. I took the lead in the conversation. Mom would reply a yes or no and sometimes a few words. We reminisced about the way God had worked in our lives. I told many of the old family stories that we knew so well, knowing she would be with Jesus one day very soon. I cherished every minute.

As my time with her came to a close, I suggested that we pray. When I reached across the table to take hold of her hands, Mom immediately began to pray in a weak, broken voice. Her words flowed much better as she talked to her Savior. That Mother's Day she prayed for God's hand to be upon each member of her family by name.

As I wiped the moisture away from my eyes, I was reminded why I needed to give my family that same kind of legacy.

What makes a strong legacy? Money, fame, happiness? Compare the lives of Robert and June.

Robert is the owner of a good size construction company in Cincinnati, with a net worth of ten million dollars. He is a good businessman, who loves his family and is known for a generous heart. As a believer, he wants to be a good example and teach his family how to walk with God.

June is a single grandmother from Denver. Her husband died when the children were young, and she never remarried. At times she needed to work two jobs just to make ends meet. Her children watched as she trusted God for their basic needs, such as rent, food, and protection. God has been faithful, and all three of her children are now serving the Lord in ministry.

On the surface, it would be easy to say Robert has the stronger legacy because he is worth ten million dollars. But should our net worth dictate our value to our family and God? If that was the case people could say, "I don't have much money, so why worry about leaving a legacy."

Nothing could be further from the truth. Your legacy is more than the money you leave behind; it's a part of you.

Legacy

Our *true* legacy is intangible. It is more about our value system and the memories we build than money. We focus on tangible items because we can see and feel them. Houses, cars, and bank accounts. But the intangible may be worth far more to our family.

Listen to the Wisdom of Solomon. "The memory of the righteous is a blessing, but the name of the wicked will rot" (Proverbs 10:7, ESV). Legacy is living. It is ongoing, even when we are not thinking about it. Each day we are building our legacy, and even after our death, our reputation, our legacy, lives on.

So how do you want to be remembered? What will people say about you fifty years from now? Will the decisions you make today influence your grandchildren? The best gift you can give your family is a living legacy. This gift will last for many generations to come. In the blogpost, *How Grandpa Influenced Me*, at doorposts.com, Daniel shared his love for his grandfather.

> "September 14 is my Grandpa's birthday. Cal Mohr has been in heaven for more than five years now, but his influence on his family and on me is still strong. He loved us, and we knew it. He helped shape who we are. When he inspired my brothers and me to build a log cabin on his property, we learned a lot about tools, trees, and American history, all while helping him accomplish one of his unfulfilled dreams. We had a blast."

My friend, Karen, discovered the importance of legacy when she researched her family's genealogy. One of her ancestors was a Cambridge-educated man named John Rogers. He became friends with William Tyndale who was translating the Bible into English. After Tyndale was martyred, John Rogers completed the manuscript and published the first English Bible in 1537 under the pseudonym, Thomas Matthew. Then he too was burned at the stake—the first of many martyrs during Queen Mary's reign. He died for the truth of God's Word. *The Matthew Bible* (as it became known) was used extensively by those who prepared the King James Bible of 1611. As Karen researched her family legacy, she discovered many preachers, missionaries, Bible scholars, and teachers, including six in her immediate family. The legacy of John Rogers who gave his life for the truth of the Word of God lives on today.

In my life, I can see the influence of a former pastor. His example taught me to expect miracles when I prayed. Pastor Don (who may be in heaven by now) had complete confidence in God's power and the Word. When he prayed, he knew God would answer that prayer. Pastor Don's legacy is still living through my life and ministry.

Our legacy is an expression of what is important to us. It is the composite of our life—even while we are still alive. One definition of legacy is "anything handed down from the past, as from an ancestor or predecessor." Synonyms for legacy are heritage and tradition. So our legacy is much more than money, it is our life, our personal history, and the values we live, teach, and pass on.

Impacting legacies do not always come from family members or close friends. Other people can influence our lives. Teachers, coaches, pastors, mentors, and sometimes even those in the political spotlight can influence us. What do you think when you hear these names and quotes.

> Dr. Martin Luther King, Jr., "I have a Dream."
> John F. Kennedy, "Ask not what your country can do for you."
> Winston Churchill, "Never give in, never give in, never, never"[1]

There are many factors that shape our values, expectations, and work ethic. The courage to live out those values during the volatile times of life produces our character. A good character is what builds a solid legacy and our footprint for God.

Don't make Money the End Game

Unfortunately, for many people, it's all about money. Since World War II, America has experienced a wealth boom. Over the past 60 years, our economy (GDP) has doubled almost every ten years. Consequently, the American dream is materialistic. Wealth is not the most important aspect of our legacy. Solomon says "A good name is to be chosen rather than great riches, and favor is better than silver or gold" (Proverbs 22:1, ESV).

So is having money wrong? Absolutely not! Money can be a blessing or a curse depending on how we use it. Many families have been blessed with great wealth and use their wealth to make our world a better place.

According to Wikipedia, the Bill & Melinda Gates Foundation is the largest private foundation in the world. Their primary focus globally is to enhance healthcare and reduce extreme poverty. "With the help of Gates-funded vaccination drives, deaths from measles in Africa have dropped by 90 percent since 2000."[2]

Wealth can also be a curse rather than a blessing. Henry Ford said, "Money doesn't change men, it merely unmasks them. If a man is naturally selfish or arrogant or greedy, the money brings that out—that's all."[3]

MC Hammer's story demonstrates that success can be a curse. At the peak of his career, his net worth was a little over $30 million. He acquired fame and fortune very quickly but lost it all and filed for bankruptcy. He was surrounded by people who were only interested in his money and not his well-being. In October 1997, MC Hammer reaffirmed his faith and later became an ordained minister.

The lesson learned—don't make money your end goal; leave a piece of yourself instead.

What about our Spiritual Legacy?

Our spiritual legacy starts with our decision to be a follower of Jesus Christ. It is built upon our relationship with God and the influence we have with the people we meet.

Billy Graham said, "The greatest legacy one can pass on to one's children and grandchildren is not money or other material things accumulated in one's life but rather a legacy of character and faith."

Through our spiritual legacy, we have the opportunity to influence our grandchildren and even the great grandchildren whom we may never meet. If we fail, we could lose our family's Christian heritage.

Paul clued us in about being a good spiritual role model. "Show yourself in all respects to be a model of good works, and in your teaching show integrity, dignity, and sound speech..." (Titus 2:7-8, ESV).

Think of your spiritual legacy as a baton that you pass to the next generation. Your children will carry that baton long after you have finished your portion of the race. Pass on your beliefs and the values that are important to you.

If you want to inspire your children to live for the Lord, then let them see your example of living by faith. Share the stories about your walk with Christ from the past and be open about what God is doing in your life right now. Let your children see the real person as you are; in the good times and when you stumble. If they see how your imperfections drive you to your knees, for a deeper walk with God, they will follow your example.

Walking by faith is especially important during your children's teenage years or if you have a child who is walking in rebellion. Stand tall for Christ, walk by faith, and live a consistent Christ-like life before them. You might be tempted to back down because of the conflict, but don't. Conflicts can cause us to doubt, but we must remain strong. Go to your knees in prayer, and search the Scriptures for guidance.

Here is an ongoing problem. Though people identify themselves as Christians and even attend church, they lack a true life of submission to Christ. They want spiritual blessings, but they want to choose when to let God in and when to go it alone. Other Christians may have a genuine commitment to Christ, but over the years the relationship has become stale. A stale relationship is almost no relationship at all.

Nothing will rob your spiritual legacy quicker than a shallow walk with God. Your children will follow you in those same footsteps. Why? They learn from us. Children can spot hypocrisy and shallowness quicker than anyone else. They see us when we are not wearing our Sunday morning smile.

Our spiritual legacy in the community is important too. We often talk about our Christian testimony as the story of how we found Christ, but our conduct can discredit our testimony. Little actions we do without giving it much thought can steal our witness for Christ and weaken our legacy. Is winning that sales contract so important that you have to stretch the truth? Do you leave work early and have someone else clock you out? If you claim to be a Christian but don't work to your full potential, your co-workers will notice, and your testimony may be wiped out.

James said we need to be above reproach. "From the same mouth come blessing and cursing. My brothers, these things ought not to be so" (James 3:10, ESV).

Intentionality

The idea of passing the baton to the next generation may be a new concept for many. For an effective handoff with our family's spiritual legacy, we need to live authentic, intentional lives. Intentional living requires a decision. It's not just hoping or trying to do our best, but it is deliberate.

Intentional living is taking the time to evaluate what we are doing each day and checking the effectiveness of our walk with God. Those decisions will affect our spiritual walk and our legacy, so make each one count. Find your purpose in life. Without knowing our true God-given purpose, we will feel unfulfilled. An unfulfilled person lacks direction and purpose. Get involved in activities that you are passionate about. Ask God how you can create a legacy while doing what you love. This is how we build our footprint for God.

In the business world, we talk about a succession plan or business legacy planning. This effort is a human attempt to keep the company in a place where it can continue to provide great service and intentionally carry on the values of the founders for many years to come. Why not think intentionally about your family? Planning your family's legacy will connect you to those before you and those whose lives you will touch in the next 100 years.

Some professionals have taken the approach of holding a family retreat or a family meeting to discuss how to keep their family's values intact. A family meeting could be as simple as a time around the kitchen table or maybe a weekend event at the lake. The larger and more complex your situation is, the more important it is to have an experienced professional assist you.

The first step in planning your family's legacy is talking about the values your family received from past generations and comparing those to your current family. Some families develop a family purpose statement or a family mission statement describing their family's priorities. Loving God and loving others, honesty, integrity, the value of education, and a strong commitment to financial integrity are just a few.

Then look forward to the next generation keeping your family's purpose alive in your family legacy. Family ministry projects engage the entire family and stimulate your family's commitment to fulfilling the Great Commission.

When it comes to making a lasting impact, Jane Wells is a shining example.

Jane received her teaching degree from Oklahoma Wesleyan University, and her first teaching job was in her hometown of Coffeyville, Kansas. She did not make much money, but she loved her job. Jane felt like each of the children from her class was part of her family. She tried to teach the children the importance of family and to honor mom and dad. Traditional values were important in this farming community.

As the world began to change, Jane felt the nudge from God to teach at a small Christian school. Even though she made less money, she had the freedom to teach biblical values to her students.

One of the highlights of her teaching career was seeing Oscar Fleming graduate with honors. Jane took Oscar under her wing after the unexpected death of his father. Watching him rebound and graduate with honors thrilled Jane.

Over the years some of her students entered into the ministry and others became outstanding leaders in Coffeyville. Now, many years later, she sees former students every week who thank her for being their best teacher.

Invest in the Eternal

"But godliness with contentment is great gain, for we brought nothing into the world, and we cannot take anything out of the world" (1 Timothy 6:6-7, ESV).

My dad used to say, "Life goes fast." When I was in my twenties, retirement years seemed so far away. It seemed I had my whole life ahead of me. Our children were young, and we struggled financially. It was a busy time in our lives. Work, school activities, and church activities had us on the go all of the time. We enjoyed many great events and made some real friends too.

It would have been easy for us to just skip church and relax or sleep in, but we didn't. With all the ball games, practices, school activities, and family outings, we still put God first. We were committed to serving God by our example of prayer, Bible study, and church activities even when we were worn out. Our goal was to let the light of Christ shine through our marriage so our children could see God at work in our home.

That commitment paid off. In the craziness of life somehow we did something right, and our children are serving the Lord today. Now I'm a grandpa, and we are blessed to have Jesus in the center of our family. Our family's spiritual legacy continues to build. Our prayer is that everything we do will continue to point our family to Christ.

When Dick Spencer made his first trip to India, he thought he was fulfilling his life-long dream of going to a third-world country to share the Gospel. While on that trip, Dick met a young pastor who had the same passion to share the gospel with the lost. With seven families in a community surrounded by Hindu temples, the two of them with God's help started Hope Evangelical Church.

A few years later they started New Hope School. The school opened its doors to the children who did not have the opportunity to get a good education. Today the church has grown to over 250 families and 350 children attending the school. The church outreach has established at least ten new churches in the surrounding villages.

Dick and Sue have invested heavily in this ministry knowing it is making a difference for eternity. When the day comes that Dick and Sue can no longer travel to India, their lasting investment will be felt for many years to come.

It Doesn't End At Our Death

For the child of God, death is not the end but our graduation. The day we pass from this life into our eternal home. Think of it this way, our witness for Christ, the time we have invested into our children and others and the example of our faith, all continue to live on, as our legacy—our footprint for God. It's not too late to make a difference. You can start today, and it won't cost you a dime. Intentional living does require you to make Godly decisions. So invest in eternal causes, and build a legacy of character and faith.

What kind of impact will we have on our society? Time will tell. Remember, our legacy does not die!

A good name is to be chosen rather than great riches.

Chapter Two

She Shaped My Life

My great grandmother was a spiritual giant and left a wonderful Christian legacy to our family. The legacy began back in 1867 near Barnstaple, England, when Harriet (Hattie) Gratton was born.

Life in Barnstaple, England

Grandma Hattie was raised in the village of Tawstock, near Barnstaple, England. A beautiful area of Southern England near the Celtic Sea. Tawstock overlooks the Taw River and is surrounded by rolling hills covered with green pastures. In Grandma Hattie's day, the population was only 1,100 people, but it was the home to one of England's most notable churches, St. Peter's Church. Grandma Hattie's father James Gratton was the church caretaker, so their family lived in the church cottage.

According to W.G. Hoskins, in his book *Devon*, "The fittings and monuments in the church are of the highest interest: an entire half-day should be allowed for their inspection."

A few years before Grandma Hattie was born, a great revival broke out in the United Kingdom beginning in Ireland. It spread to Wales, Scotland and all of England. This move of God became known as the Great Awakening in Liverpool. "By 1864 no less than 600,000 people were converted in England, bringing the total in the UK to over one million people."[4]

Her Life in America

As a 17-year-old, she migrated from England to the United States with her older brother. Like many, they searched for opportunity. She met my great-grandfather, William Edwards, in Peoria, Illinois, and they were married in 1889.

During the Great Depression, they lived on a small farm in rural South Dakota. Their home was a one-room farmhouse with no electricity, no running water and a pot-belly stove for heat. Hattie and William raised several of their grandchildren in that one-room house. One of those grandchildren was my dad.

They were poor. My dad remembers when they couldn't buy coal for heat, so they burned corn instead. Even though the corn was worth two cents a bushel, they couldn't sell it because no one had money to buy it even at that price.

As a ten-year-old boy, my dad was embarrassed when they nailed tin on the bottom of his shoes because of the holes he had worn in them. They could not afford new shoes or have them repaired, so tin was the only choice. My dad said his shoes clicked like tap-dancing shoes when he walked.

Even with all those difficult memories, my dad remembers the legacy of Grandma Hattie. Her Christian life left a lasting impression on his young mind.

Her Christian Influence

The nearest church was about 10 miles away in the town of Hecla, South Dakota, so they didn't get to church very often. So Grandma Hattie taught Sunday School in that one-room house—for the grandchildren and the other nearby children. In the summertime, she organized a Summer Bible School for their entire farming community.

Grandma Hattie was a teetotaler (a total abstainer) and very active in the Temperance Movement. As a devoted Christian, she fought the use of alcohol in any form. Even though the Temperance Movement had begun to lose some of its momentum, she was still a strong supporter.

Dad told me about one Saturday night when Grandma Hattie heard that the neighbor boys had built a still and were making moonshine. That spunky lady went down to the next farm and busted up that still!

Early the next morning, she had the nerve to go back to that same farmhouse and beat on the door to wake everybody up. She said, "Get out here and hitch up those horses, and take us into town for church!"

Grandma Hattie's influence was the main reason why my dad committed his life to Christ. Our family serves the Lord because of Grandma Hattie's legacy and her faithfulness to God.

Even now—100 years later—her legacy is still evident in our family. Now it's my turn to leave a legacy so that 100 years from now our great-grandchildren will know why Nana & Papa Edwards stood for the Lord.

My Decision for Christ

During the early years of my life, my mom and dad became involved in a mainline denominational church. It was a good church, but the gospel was not clearly presented. I considered myself a Christian because I was at church every Sunday. I had been baptized as an infant and joined the church in my pre-teen years, but I did not have a personal relationship with Christ. I knew about God in my head, but I had not surrendered my life to His control.

In September 1970, I was invited to a Campus Life Club meeting in our school. It was the organizational meeting for the new school year, and somehow I was elected as the vice-president of the club. When the first meeting day arrived, I attended since I was an officer.

The Bible study that night was from the third chapter of John—the story of Nicodemus. One night Nicodemus came to Jesus with some spiritual questions. Jesus said, "Very truly I tell you, no one can see the kingdom of God unless they are born again" (John 3:3).

After the meeting was over the leader asked me what I thought of the lesson. My response was, "It was good."

Then he dropped the bombshell, "Would you say you are born again?"

I said, "Well I've been a good person. I have been baptized, and I'm a church member." *After all, wasn't that enough?*

The leader of the Bible study wisely said, "Kenn, that's not what I asked. Have you ever been born again like Nicodemus?" Then he asked, "Was there a time when your spiritual life began?"

As I thought about it, I realized I was trying to be a good person and earn eternal life by my good works. I had heard people say, "I know he is in Heaven because he was a good person." But at that moment, the words of Jesus and Nicodemus made sense. I would never be worthy of His love on my good works, and my religious acts were not enough. So that night I prayed a simple prayer, asking Jesus to forgive my sins and give me the gift of eternal life.

What had been missing was a personal relationship with Christ; a spiritual life. Over the next six months, my life changed. For the first time in my life, I wanted to go to a Bible study to learn about God and His love for me.

Around that same time our church received a new pastor who knew what a life with Christ was all about. His passion for Christ was contagious, and our family experienced a spiritual renewal. Over the next few years my Dad, Mom, and I served on several Lay Witness Missions teams in various cities, and I went on my first international mission trip to Colombia, South America. God radically changed our family.

Spiritual Influence

Who in your walk with God has been the influencer for you? Someone who inspired you to go deeper with God? A friend or a family member who has been consistent in their walk with God regardless of their situation? Someone who asked you the hard questions? Someone who taught you the truth?

LifeWay published the article, "Who Is Your Spiritual Hero?" They had collected stories from students about the person whom they consider their spiritual influence. Alicia Claxton shared her story about her dad, David.

"His faith impacted every aspect of his life—as a husband, father, friend, and pastor. He went to be with the Lord when I was in college, but his influence in the years I had with him lingers on. I recently wrote down a few memories of him that have shaped my life and character.

My dad never met a stranger and could strike up a conversation with just about anyone. I remember one time, in particular, we were standing in line at Disney World (before the days of Fast Passes) when he started befriending the people in line around us. Before long, they were swapping life stories and asking spiritual questions.

My dad ended up sharing the gospel with a small crowd right outside the entrance to Space Mountain. I think at the time I might have been embarrassed that my dad was always in "preacher mode," but later in life I realized something: he didn't share the gospel because he was a preacher, he told people about Jesus because he never got over the beautiful gift of grace."[5]

Each day we influence people around us without thinking about it. Our life should reflect a powerful message that Jesus Christ has changed my life.

What if the 12 disciples had not evangelized? What if the early church fathers had failed at their mission to establish the church? What if the Jewish leaders were right and Christianity died out. Praise God; the New Testament Church that started on the Day of Pentecost continues to grow today. From 12 disciples to 2.18 billion Christians in the world today according to Pew Research.[6] This growth did not happen by accident. The church grew because of the work of the Holy Spirit in the hearts of men and women just like you and me.

Growing in our relationship with God is important. Growing keeps our relationship fresh and alive with our Lord. If we are not growing in Christ, the world is chipping away at the foundation. Our spiritual legacy could crumble.

As a young man, I drove a school bus to provide extra income for our family. We lived in a small rural community, and the countryside was filled with farmhouses and rolling hills. Each day I saw streams, creeks, and farm ponds along my bus route. There was one disgusting farm pond covered with green algae. It was nothing more than a mosquito farm. At first, I observed the pond and wondered why it was so different. Why wasn't the water clear? Over the next several weeks I continued to observe that pond with great curiosity.

Then one day I noticed it was a man-made pond and did not have a stream flowing through it. That pond never gave; it only took water in and never let any water out. It trapped all the water that came in. It was a self-centered pond. With no way to cleanse itself, the pond was stale and unfit for life.

Don't let your spiritual life be like that stagnant pond; give yourself away and let the Holy Spirit refill you with His love. This is the best way to build your Christian Legacy and your footprint for God.

Fred Kawaski

Fred Kawaski is one of those guys with a strong Christian testimony. Fred and his wife Joan have three children and own a pharmacy in a small town in Wisconsin. To many of the townspeople, Fred is a hero. Fred says he is just doing his job servicing his customers. His pharmacy is the only one for 20 miles, so everyone depends on him when an emergency arises. One night when Bessie Johnson needed some medication at 3:00 a.m., Fred drove through a snow storm to take the medication to her house.

Fred takes his faith seriously. In addition to being an elder in his church, he teaches a men's interdenominational Bible study. Occasionally he will preach the Sunday message when the pastor is out of town. Fred has been a city council member for the past 20 years and tries to be a real Christian example in the community.

One of his greatest blessings has been to see their daughter marry a young missionary and relocate to the Philippines. Even though they are 8,000 miles apart, they stay in touch by email and video phone calls.

Fred and Joan are thankful for the Christian legacy given to them. They feel blessed because their children have continued that legacy and are serving the Lord.

Keeping it Alive

How do I keep a lasting legacy alive for my grandchildren without spending a lot of money? Here are several simple ideas that will remind your family of their heritage.

Tell stories from the past. Stories are a great tool to keep the family history embedded in the minds of our children. Everybody loves a story especially the details. Stories that we hear over and over again become a part of our lives too. Research suggests our brains become more active when we tell stories. Maybe that's why a good story captivates us.

Assemble picture books and scrapbooks. You have heard it said "A picture is worth a thousand words" so why not create memory books? Scan those old pictures and upload them into one of the online services with print-on-demand capabilities. To print a book like this is relatively easy and cost effective. Scrapbooking is making a comeback. It too is an easy way to build a memory book from invitations, announcements, and public notices.

Capture the stories on paper or in a blog. If we are not careful, we can forget some of the important details of our family history. Creating a journal for your favorite family stories will give you a written record to pass to the next generation. A trendy way to accomplish the same goal while sharing it with your friends and family is through an online blog.

Keep those funny situations alive. Every family has some hilarious moments like this story from our family. One summer when I was about seven years old we were traveling. We stopped for a picnic lunch at a roadside park. As my mom scurried around getting our picnic lunch on the table, my sister and I sat down to eat. Soon Dad joined us. When Mom completed her tasks, she sat down on the picnic table bench right next to my dad. The only problem was all four of us were on the same side of the picnic table. Within a matter of seconds, the off-balanced picnic table flipped right over on top of us! We were all sitting on the ground, and our lunch was in our laps! Memories like these will keep a family laughing together for many years to come!

Live your passions. Pastor TD Jakes said, "It is your passion that empowers you to be able to do that thing you were created to do."[7] God designed every one of us to live with passion, energy, and a strong desire for something BIG in life. If we are living in the area where God has made us passionate, it shows.

Teach true success. Teach your family what true success means—it's more than money. Show them how to give themselves away so our world will be a better place. Leave a little bit of your heart; this is true success.

How do I keep my spiritual legacy alive and build my footprint for God? It all starts with our example of faithfulness. There is nothing like a consistent walk with God to strengthen our reputation, our testimony, and our spiritual legacy. Lasting impact happens when Jesus Christ is Lord of our lives.

Set the believers an example in speech, in conduct, in love, in faith, in purity.

Chapter Three

Deeper

Have you ever known a person who is driven? Someone who will do practically anything to succeed. Not long ago, I was in a hotel fitness room. As I was walking on the treadmill, I watched a 30-year-old man drenched in sweat and gasping for air. He was pushing himself as if there was a drill sergeant, breathing down his neck, yelling at him to push harder and harder. What I observed was passion.

Passion

Passion in life is good. Especially if that passion points people to Christ. Passion comes from a strong, heartfelt desire to achieve. A businessman is driven by making money. Artists are driven to perform because of the fame. Athletes like this man are driven by the need to win.

Those observations make me ask, "Am I passionate about God?" Does my passion drive me into a deeper relationship with Him? Am I willing to study my Bible even when I'm drenched in sweat and gasping for air? Why not? We have time, energy, and money for other passions. What about our passion for Christ?

More than Superficial

Our goal should be a deeper walk with God, not a superficial life. We miss so much when our walk with God is shallow. He longs for daily fellowship with each one of us. That is why we were created.

But here is the dichotomy. According to Pew Research, there are 2.18 billion[8] Christians on earth—the highest at any time in history. At the same time, Barna Research says in the United States, of those identifying themselves as born-again Christians, less than 9% have a biblical worldview[9]. Why is there a disconnect between someone who wears the label of Christian and someone who uses the Bible as a guidebook for living a Christian life?

Let's look first at the definition of biblical worldview. Christian researcher, George Barna, says there are six core biblical beliefs in a biblical worldview: the accuracy of the Bible, the sinless nature of Jesus, the literal existence of Satan, God is all knowing, and all power, salvation by grace alone, and each has the personal responsibility to evangelize. In addition to these six core doctrines, a biblical worldview includes the belief in absolute moral truth as defined by Scripture.[10] Simply put, a biblical worldview believes what God said in His Word and considers the Bible as the foundation of life. For Christians, a biblical worldview is critical, because if the Word of God is not reliable, then we do not have much hope for forgiveness or eternal life.

Let's unpack this disconnect further. First, we must be careful to distinguish between religion and a relationship with Christ. People who are steeped in religion try to fulfill their Christian obligation by going to church. They may talk about religious symbols, ceremonies, and the liturgy, but many feel the Bible is not relevant in daily life—so they struggle with the idea of a biblical worldview.

Christians with a relationship with Christ are more likely to talk about how Jesus has changed their life. This type of relationship is different than any other relationship. While it is similar to an earthly relationship with your spouse or another close family member, it is a relationship with God through prayer. Our relationship with God is strengthened as we spend time studying the Bible (God's Word to man), and learning how to become more like Christ every day. Having a relationship like this with Christ is the most important aspect of our Christianity. Our church attendance, baptism, church membership, and giving, are all birthed out of that relationship—not an obligation.

Another phenomenon that has shaped the spiritual climate in the United States is the availability of the Gospel. But just because someone knows about God does not mean they have a relationship with God.

One night Jim watched an evangelist on television. He felt guilty because of an affair he was having. When the preacher prayed, Jim said those same words. He thought he was a Christian, but there was no change in his lifestyle, and he never developed a relationship with Christ.

Julie feels she is a Christian because morally she is a good person. She attended a parochial school as a kid but wants nothing to do with church today. She may have the label as a Christian, but is there a relationship with Christ?

The true test is whether we are walking in obedience to God and His Word. Each one of us should know the time when we turned our life over to God by faith, asking Him for eternal life. God's desire is for us to come to Christ as we are and grow to be like Him; that is a relationship with God.

Gary is a bricklayer from northeast Ohio. Because of the cold winters he spent most of his downtime at the local tavern—a place where he could be around people and not feel alone. Since the death of his younger brother, Gary felt awkward and lonesome.

Last summer Gary met Juan as they worked on the same brick laying crew. Gary admired Juan's hard work and his sincere work ethic. He was unlike most of the bricklayers Gary knew, and his daddy was a preacher.

One day Juan invited Gary to attend a Fourth of July celebration and fireworks at his church. The patriotic music reminded Gary of his childhood. When Juan's father stood up to preach, he said "Our freedom was not free. Many men gave their lives to provide the freedom we enjoy today." Gary remembered his little brother who was killed in the Iraq war. While he was very sad, he also felt happy his brother gave his life protecting our country.

Juan's father continued. He said, "Because of the sacrifice of Jesus Christ on the cross we can have true freedom." After the program, Gary and Juan prayed together, and Gary committed his life to Christ.

As Gary looks back at the past two years, he sees how God used Juan in his life. Now his life is totally different because of his relationship with Christ. He doesn't spend time at the tavern because Juan's church became his new family. Gary is thankful for that July 4th when he met Jesus Christ as his Savior, and he discovered true freedom.

Our footprint for God and our spiritual legacy depends on a strong relationship with the Lord. If you want to have a lasting spiritual impact, seek a deeper walk with God. Live with passion for God, and let Jesus Christ be the Lord of your life. If you are like Joshua, who said, "as for me and my house we, will serve the Lord" you will give an inheritance to your children that money cannot buy.

Greater Impact

I love a ride on an open road. Especially on a beautiful springtime day with the warmth of the sunshine filling the car. Now imagine riding down the road at 70 mph with the steering wheel shaking back and forth because of bad tires. With a quick trip to the tire shop, the car is fixed. The mechanic says, "Small things make a big difference." He explains how a small, one-ounce wheel weight keeps your tires in balance.

For us to have a greater impact we need to watch the small stuff in our spiritual life too. Without realizing it, life can get out of balance just like the tires on the car. The need to *fit-in* can quickly deflate our tires before we are aware of the slightest change. Peer pressure in this modern world could cause us to second guess our faith and deny the truth of God's Word. The world says many of our traditional Christian values are out of date. That same need to *fit-in* might lead us to socialize with groups or activities that tear down our belief system instead of building it up. When this happens, it dampens our spiritual growth and damages our Christian legacy.

To keep our life in balance, Christ should be the pivot-point of our life—the absolute center. Everything should revolve around Him. He designed the best plan for our lives before we were born. Our job is to follow His plan.

Following can be harder than we think because we want to be in control. We have two choices. Either we allow Christ to sit on the throne as King of Kings, or we usurp His authority. When we seize authority, we say, "God, it's my life. I'll live it my way." Then we keep God on the sidelines so we can call on Him for an emergency—just in case.

Straddling the fence, between the world and the Christian life causes conflicts because we are too close to sin. Our lifestyle may hinder our relationship with God. Choices that are totally acceptable in today's society may be completely unacceptable or offensive to Him. Last year a large Albuquerque church sponsored a teaching series on marriage. At the end of the series, they challenged the couples living together outside of marriage to tie-the-knot in obedience to God's Word. Though the societal norm was one way, the church chose to follow God.

True Purpose

To find our true purpose in life, we need to live with passion for our Lord. One of the definitions for passion is hunger and thirst. King David understood, "O God, you are my God; earnestly I seek you; my soul thirsts for you; my flesh faints for you, as in a dry and weary land where there is no water" (Psalm 63:1, ESV).

Remember the 30-year-old man, absolutely drenched in sweat and gasping for air because he was so driven to win? As I think of him, I wonder, "How do I develop that kind of passion in my life for the Lord?"

There are two words commonly used in Scripture for passion: zeal and fervor. Paul instructed the Roman Christians, "Never be lacking in zeal, but keep your spiritual fervor, serving the Lord" (Romans 12:11).

Zeal means to have great energy or enthusiasm in pursuit of a cause or an objective. That's why many of the old-timers would describe zeal as the *fire of God burning in my bones*. Fervor is defined as a strong feeling of excitement and enthusiasm.

Energy, excitement, and enthusiasm are all necessary in our work for the Lord. Passion is like a fire. Passion is found in the power of the Holy Spirit. When we allow the Holy Spirit to work in our lives, He fans the flames so the fire will burn. Paul reminded the young preacher Timothy, "For this reason I remind you to fan into flame the gift of God, which is in you…" (2 Timothy 1:6). Did the zeal of God burn within you as a new believer? Is that zeal still burning in your bones today? Go back and revisit why you made the decision to follow Christ. Remind yourself what God has done in you.

Many of us can remember the early days in our adventure with God. Because of our zeal we would do anything for the Lord. If someone invited us to go work with the homeless, we were excited to share what Christ had done. We need to rekindle that fire for God again.

If you have never experienced God in this way, don't worry. Today is a great day to get a fresh start with God. These principles will apply to anyone who wants a dynamic life with Christ.

Don't settle for status quo. It is easy to fall into the trap of letting life happen instead of getting engaged for the Lord. When our Bible sits on the shelf, and we forget to pray, our spiritual tank runs dry. How can we have passion for God with an empty tank? Spiritual fervor says, get involved where you are and let God use you. God wants you to be engaged in work for the Kingdom of God.

Realize we are in a battle. Our adversary the devil continually seeks to trip-up believers. Every day we encounter demonic forces in our lives. They want to keep us discouraged, disengaged, and sitting on the sideline. God's zeal puts us in the heat of the battle, but remember, "the battle is not yours but God's" (2 Chronicles 20:15, ESV). This battle is real, so don't succumb to the lies of Satan.

Fellowship with other believers. People influence us, building our faith or tearing it down. Our small group is important in our spiritual growth. In a good small group, we will connect with other believers for encouragement, prayer support, and accountability as we grow in our Christian walk.

Phil is the leader of a discipleship group in Tennessee. He invited Jason his neighbor over to the house to meet his group. Jason had recently gone through a divorce and was still dealing with the shock of it all. As the leader, Phil was so pleased the way the group accepted Jason. By the end of the night, he was laughing and carrying on like he knew everyone. A few weeks later Jason finally began to open up to the group about his situation. Much to his surprise, there were two others from the group who had been through a difficult divorce. Their encouragement gave Jason hope that God still cared for him.

A small group is an excellent place for us to sow into the lives of others. When we give of ourselves, it builds our legacy and teaches the next generation of leaders.

Grasp the larger picture. Have you ever dreamed of wiping out hunger, taking care of the orphans of the world, or feeding all the homeless in your city? God has placed those desires in your life for a reason. Start with one—one orphan, one homeless person, and see how God can use you to reach more.

Gregg loves kids. He is the kind that always see their potential, and he encourages the children to excel at everything they do. Many years before, a group from Compassion International came to their church. That night Gregg sponsored his first child. When he received the first letter from Carlos, it changed his life. Because of his passion for children he now sponsors ten children in Guatemala. Two years ago he had the privilege of traveling to Guatemala to meet his kids! Gregg knows that his connection with these children is making an eternal difference.

Remember, you are not here by accident. He has a plan to use you to change the world one person at a time.

Talk to God. A relationship requires communication. Paul said, "Pray without ceasing," so have an attitude of prayer all day long—as you walk, clean house, or mow the grass—talk to God. Develop the discipline of systematic prayer. Everyday, at the same time, make it a habit to meet with God via prayer. Many people like to keep a journal so they can remember how God answered their prayers.

Stretch your faith. Because we have so many solutions in our country, it becomes easy to live without much faith. When faith is not required our faith muscle turns to flab. Miracles and answered prayer come by exercising our faith. When we trust God and see Him miraculously answer prayer, our faith grows—that gives us fresh energy to share Christ. So live on the edge and let God work through you.

Study the Scripture. Although reading or listening to the Bible is very good, studying the Bible develops a deeper understanding. A Bible study is a great place to start, especially if you have a good teacher. Prepare for each lesson in advance even if you are not leading the group. You will be amazed how the Bible comes alive as a seamless book from Genesis to Revelation. Then plan to teach a Bible study or take part in the lesson. It is amazing how much more you will learn by preparing to teach the class. Over time you will have a greater understanding and a much better appreciation for the Word of God.

Share your faith. What better way is there to build a legacy than to have spiritual grandchildren. Share your story of how God has changed you. It's your story, so it will be easy to share with those that God brings into your life. As we grow in our walk with Christ, we will be a witness to others by our example and by the words of our testimony.

Develop a personal ministry. It is good to be involved in a community-based ministry. When you are connected with believers from various churches, you will have a better understanding of the Body of Christ. Every community has outreach programs to help the homeless, collect backpacks for school children, wrap Christmas Shoeboxes, or many other causes. Go on a mission trip if you want to turn your spiritual life upside down for the good. Follow the desire that God has given to you. You will grow in God's grace and learn to impact those around you.

Best Gift

During our lifetime our family depends on us. Even if we now live in another city or state, our family needs us to be their rock and example. As parents, the best gift we can leave our family is the legacy of walking with God. Model the lifestyle of a believer with our time, talent, and our finances.

Your footprint for God will be evident long after you have reached your heavenly home. It encompasses everything that God has given to you. Teach your children to be good stewards of their time, talents, and their finances, because everything is a gift from God.

That I may know him and the power of his resurrection.

Chapter Four

It's not Mine

They said it couldn't be done, but Stanley Tam made God the owner of his business. In 1955, while watching people at the altar in front of the church, God asked Mr. Tam, "If a soul is the greatest value in all the world, then what investment can you make that will pay you the greatest dividends a hundred years from now?"[11]

Stanley Tam was already giving 60% of the income from U.S. Plastic Corporation, but on January 15, 1955, he told God that he would give the entire business to God. Today his businesses are large and profitable, giving several million dollars annually to the Lord's work. Mr. Tam found the secret to business success—give it to God!

Stanley Tam's legacy will pay dividends many years after his death—reaching thousands of people every year with the Good News of Jesus Christ. Stanley Tam understood that everything belonged to God.

Biblical Stewardship
A proper understanding of stewardship helps keep our life in balance. Stewardship is about God's ownership.

The story of Stanley Tam is counterculture for most Americans. In reality, this idea is biblical. Our typical reaction might be: *I worked hard to earn everything I have—my car, my house, and my bank account. It was my blood, sweat, and tears.* Or *Doesn't God only require my tithe?*

The influence from our society doesn't help either. The American dream has become materialistic, obsessed with getting more and more. We not only believe we deserve wealth because of our hard work, but we believe our success is ours to do with as we desire.

Statistically, the Christian church is no different than the general public in the way we handle money. We love our prosperity, our designer clothes, and our latte too. We work long hours and strap ourselves with debt so we can have more to enjoy. The irony is that we work so hard, we have little free time left to enjoy the stuff.

Alex and Erin

Alex is a young engineer in the Atlanta Metro area, and Erin is the office manager at a small medical office. In addition to these demanding jobs, they are active in their church and try to keep up with all the activities of their three children. Both of them want to provide a strong spiritual environment and foundation for the family. It seems they work night and day to get everything done. By the time they get home, have dinner, and help the kids finish their homework, it is nearly bedtime.

Since they both have good jobs, they own a five-bedroom house in a classy subdivision. Alex recently received a nice bonus from his company, so he splurged and bought himself a new sports car. They feel blessed.

One Sunday morning, the pastor preached from Psalms 50:10 "He [God] owns the cattle on a thousand hills." Then the pastor said, "All belongs to God. That house you think you own? It is God's. That car you just bought? Belongs to God."

Alex felt the words burn into his mind. His first reaction was anger, "Hey, I work hard and I deserve that car!" Then he decided the Pastor must not mean "all." Surely, he meant that we are to give back a portion to God. He thought, *I tithe, that's all God expects.*

Owning a sports car is not a problem. In fact, a shiny sports car sounds exciting, and one of our family members recently bought one. The real question is, how do we make decisions about the way we spend our money.

Recognizing It's Not Mine

If we took a survey next Sunday at your church asking, "Do you know that God owns everything?" A high percentage of your fellow Christians would say, "Yes God owns it all." This concept has been an accepted teaching in the church for years.

Many of those same churchgoers who believe God owns it all, spend money as if it was their own. We make financial decisions every day, and we rarely consult God about the way we spend our money.

We know God owns it all, but somehow there is a disconnect between our head and our heart. Intellectually (in our head) we believe God owns it all, but for some reason knowing this fact has not changed the way we live; this concept has never truly penetrated our heart.

So whose is it? God's or ours?

Ultimately everything we have is from God. We may have purchased it with the money from our bank account, but it is God who gave us the ability to earn a living. So stewardship is managing the property that God has entrusted to us.

Have you ever had an experience like this?

You hear about a new car model that is available at the dealership. So you say, I am going to check it out.

When you step on the showroom floor, a young lady approaches you to see if she can help. You inquire about the car and take it for a test drive. The new car smell, the clean, fresh interior, and the bright shiny finish excite you. It is what you have been looking for. You feel you must buy this car.

When they calculate the trade-in value of your old car, your heart leaps for joy because it is doable. The payment is only $50 per month more. So you call your spouse and explain the great deal they offered you. After a few minutes, your spouse gives you the okay to buy the car. You complete the deal and drive the new car home that day to show it to all of your friends and neighbors.

How often has something similar happened to you? We make decisions using logic and hopefully common sense, but we don't ask God for wisdom.

God has equipped our minds with amazing capabilities. Our minds are like computers, processing information at lightning speed. We make several thousand decisions every day almost without thinking. Unfortunately all too often, we make important decisions without seeking the guidance of the Holy Spirit.

Life of Stewardship
So why should I include God in the financial decisions of my life?

First, it is God who gives you the strength, knowledge, and ability to earn a living. "You shall remember the Lord your God, for it is he who gives you power to get wealth, that he may confirm his covenant that he swore to your fathers, as it is this day" (Deuteronomy 8:18, ESV).

We were designed by God to work and lead a productive life. We may take this for granted, but God is the one who gave us our health, mental capacity, and stamina to work every day. He also gives us the intellect to save money and the desire to accumulate the possessions we call our wealth.

Even in the Garden of Eden, God told Adam to work the Garden and take care of it. It was a natural part of his life. God designed us so that we feel complete through our work. When we are not able to work, or even worse when we do not want to work, we feel unfulfilled. We find significance through our work, and our work provides the income we need. Even if you are a stay-at-home parent, you receive satisfaction through the work of taking care of your home and family.

The second part of God's covenant with man is to bless us so He (God) can reveal His glory in the world. Look at the latter part of Deuteronomy 8:18, "...he who gives you power to get wealth, that he may confirm his covenant that he swore to your fathers, as it is this day."

Remember the words that God spoke to Abram (Abraham) about the covenant? "And I will make of you a great nation, and I will bless you and make your name great, so that you will be a blessing...¹n you all the families of the earth shall be blessed" (Genesis 12:2-3, ESV).

When God's children walk in His blessings, it reveals His power to the world. But when we are strapped with debt and live paycheck to paycheck, we loose the ability to go, do, and give in support of God's Kingdom work. His plan is that every part of our life points people to Christ. When our plan is out of balance with God's plan, the Kingdom of God suffers.

Manager of God's Stuff

So it is important to remember that all of our material possessions are blessings from God. His plan is for us to use it wisely, to multiply it, and use it for His glory. When we do this, Christ is lifted up, and the world will know that we serve the one true living God.

The best example of this concept in Scripture is found in the parable of the talents (Matthew 25). A parable is a story with a truth embedded in it. In this parable, a master called three of his servants in to see him and gave money to each one of them.

"For it will be like a man going on a journey, who called his servants and entrusted to them his property. To one he gave five talents, to another two, to another one, to each according to his ability. Then he went away" (Matthew 25:14-15, ESV).

Each talent represented a lot of money; some calculate that each talent was equivalent to 20 years of wages for the average worker of that day. In today's dollars, one talent is worth about $800,000.

The master gave each servant the talents expecting him to put it to good use and care for the master's money just as he (the master) would have. In fact, when the master returned he was expecting to get more than he had given to each servant.

According to Scripture, when the master came back, he asked each servant to give an account of what they had done with the money.

The servant with five talents put the master's property to work. "He who had received the five talents went at once and traded with them, and he made five talents more" (Matthew 25:16, ESV). The master commended the servant for his hard work, wise choices, and effective management of the master's resources. "His master said to him, 'Well done, good and faithful servant. You have been faithful over a little; I will set you over much. Enter into the joy of your master'" (Matthew 25:23, ESV).

The servant with two talents put them to work and doubled the master's property. His master said to him, "Well done, good and faithful servant."

But then the master called the servant with one talent, a slothful servant because he hid the master's money. The master was upset, "…you ought to have invested my money with the bankers, and at my coming I should have received what was my own with interest" (Matthew 25:27, ESV).

While there are several truths to learn from this parable, the main point is the master trusted the servants with his money and expected them to manage it wisely.

Using Everything for His Glory

As we begin to see God's plan for our lives, then we will recognize we are stewards and God is the owner. Clinging too tightly to our earthly possessions takes the focus off God and puts it back on us. Once we finally recognize God's ownership and gladly accept it, stewardship makes a lot more sense. Our desire should be to hear those words "well done" with everything God has put into our care. God sees the big picture and knows what is best for us even better than we know ourselves. Back in 2008 in the middle of the Great Recession, we were making the transition to Albuquerque. Our house was for sale, and it seemed as if the financial world was collapsing around us. I was driving through the corn fields of Illinois when the government announced that the big New York bank, Lehman Brothers would be allowed to go bankrupt (September 15, 2008). I wondered if there would be a banking system in place so we could sell our house.

I remembered crying out to God saying, "You have called us to Albuquerque, please give me wisdom about what we should do." Each day we continued to pray, and we believed. Within two weeks we had a contract on our home, and it closed 30 days later without any problems. God had everything under control, and my job was to trust Him even when things seemed impossible. If I had panicked, the plan to move to Albuquerque might have failed.

God's Plan

God has blessed you and me financially for three reasons. First, to meet our needs—not everything that we want, but everything that is necessary to care for our families. Next, God wants us to put our finances to work and multiply it; as in the parable of the talents. Then God blesses us so we can release more resources for Kingdom work.

Remember Alex? When he got home from church that Sunday, he went into the garage to take a look at his new sports car. He grabbed the microfiber chamois and began to polish the hood. He loved this car, the bold color, the sleek lines, and especially the powerful engine designed to go from 0-50 in under 4.9 seconds. It had always been his dream to own a car like this. As he buffed, he struggled, *Does God want my car? Doesn't he love me enough to let me keep it?*

When Erin came into the garage, she asked, " What are you doing?"

"I've been thinking about what Pastor said today. Do you think God is pleased that I bought this car?"

Erin answered, "I don't know. I hadn't thought of it like that."

Every day we make decisions without giving it a thought. If God is the owner and we are His stewards, we must be willing to submit to His Lordship with everything.

> *God owns it all and we are His stewards.*
> *Our part is to practice good Stewardship.*

Chapter Five

Blessed to be a Blessing

If God is the owner and I am His steward, that changes everything. Now I must ask myself; why has God blessed me? How is my footprint for God related to stewardship?

We may not realize this, but most Americans are in the wealthiest 3% of the world. That is hard for us to comprehend. We have become so accustomed to our lifestyle that we have lost touch with the rest of the world. Just stop and think—50% of the world lives on $2.00 a day or less. Jesus said, "...it is easier for a camel to go through the eye of a needle than for a rich person to enter the kingdom of God" (Matthew 19:24, ESV).

Surprise in Africa

It was an experience that I'll never forget. The year was 1995—my first trip to Africa. We landed late at night in Ouagadougou. We drove to the hotel in the dark. The next morning I rose early so I could get a glimpse of the capital city of Burkina Faso.

As I pulled back what appeared to be an old bedspread hung across the window, I was surprised to see dirt streets for roads in the capital city. Across the street from my hotel was a street market in full swing selling goats, chickens, fruit, and other foods I didn't recognize. Everything was covered with flies and dirt.

Our driver came early to pick us up because we had to travel about 100 kilometers to the first village. Along the way, I saw the grass huts that I had envisioned in the countryside. The mud huts had no electricity, no running water, and no inside toilets. Much to my amazement, I found people who were happy, even though they did not have all the things of life that I was accustomed too.

The lesson I learned is that money doesn't bring happiness. In the villages of Haiti, the slums in India, the dirt streets of Burkina Faso, people are poor, yet they have happiness. In America, from the plains of the Midwest to the shores of the Pacific, or on the busy streets of a major city, people are rich yet can't find happiness.

What is Happiness?

In 2013 Harvard released the details of the Grant Study. A-75 year research project into what makes people happy. The Huffington Post published their findings in an article, The *75-Year Study That Found The Secrets To A Fulfilling Life*.[12] The study observed 268 Harvard graduates over a 75-year period.

According to the Harvard study on a Fulfilled Life, the most important factor was, *Love Is Really All That Matters*. The participants in this research realized that love is the key to happiness, fulfillment, and significance.

The ability to love is something God embedded in each of us. Not the emotional feeling of love, but something much deeper. Every human has an innate need to be loved and give love in return. Giving of ourselves brings completeness and fulfillment in our life.

Unfortunately, most of the world looks for love in all the wrong places. We chase the emotional side of love looking for significance. When it does not meet our expectations, we look for something else to fill that void. Chasing the void can lead us down a path of disappointment, heartache, and loneliness. The simplicity of love is a mystery that many miss.

God's love is the most important love. His love is unfailing and extends to us regardless of who we are or where we are in life. In God's Word, we discover how to love our family, those around us, and the unlovable too. None of us deserve His love, but because of His grace, He loves us.

The second finding was, *It's About More than Money and Power*. Imagine these Harvard graduates who are ambitious and motivated to be successful. When they reached the pinnacle of success with riches and power, these participants discovered the truth: life is not found in the abundance of things.

Our happiness does not come from acquiring more; it comes through living our lives with purpose. The reason some of us always want more and more is to fill the emptiness that is in our hearts. When we miss God's purpose for our lives, we feel incomplete. But when we find our purpose and allow God to direct our steps, others will be changed for eternity. That's how we find completeness and fulfillment.

But the blessings of God are not automatic. There is a price to be paid, and that price is submission to the Lord. Each day we build our spiritual legacy as we become the hands and feet of Christ.

Being the Hands and Feet of Christ

Each of us has a sweet spot in serving that makes our life meaningful. That sweet spot may be serving in a local ministry, working on a mission project, teaching children, serving in a homeless ministry, loving on senior adults or evangelism. Whatever your sweet spot of joy is, find it! That is the place where you can walk in contentment and experience the joy of the Lord!

Jan and her husband are involved with the Gideons in Colorado. During her nursing career, God used Jan many times to be the hands and feet of Christ as she cared for her patients. One night while working her shift, Jan received a call from the operating room. They were sending her team a critically ill patient. The doctor said to keep him as comfortable as possible because he was not expected to live through the night.

When he arrived, he was awake and crying because the doctor told him he didn't have a chance. Jan saw this as golden opportunity to comfort him and share the hope of Christ with him too. She took her little white New Testament designed for nurses and asked him if she could read one of the Psalms and pray with him. Some of Jan's coworkers also came into his room and they prayed for him to be comfortable and to put his trust in the Lord. Jan laid her New Testament by him and said, "We will take turns reading to you through the night."

The next morning he was no longer crying, and he even had a grin on his face. As she was going off duty, he asked, "Can I keep your little book?" Jan was thrilled.

His care went on for several days as he grew stronger and stronger. Finally, Jan had a weekend off, and when she came back on Monday night, the staff was waiting for her. She became concerned and wondered if he had died over the weekend. Jan said, "Well, I was wrong." He was waiting for her with a big hug. Since he was going home the next day, Jan encouraged him to look for a Bible teaching church, and he promised that he would.

Serving others creates a platform to share our faith and teach others how to walk with our Lord. There is no better way to build our spiritual legacy than by giving of ourselves. "For even the Son of Man came not to be served but to serve, and to give his life as a ransom for many."

C. T. Studd was a missionary to China, who was hand picked by Hudson Taylor in the late 1800s. In addition to his missionary work he loved to write. One of his most well-loved sayings is:

> Only one life 'twill soon be past.
>
> Only what's done for Christ will last.[13]

Stewardship and Our Legacy

The next step in becoming a good steward is asking ourselves, why has God trusted me? How does God want to use the income and assets entrusted to me to be a blessing to others?

Stewardship covers every area of our lives: time, talent, and yes our finances. It even includes our interests, opportunities, talents, and spiritual gifting. But that stuff we think is ours consumes us and gets in the way. It clutters up our lives. The drive to succeed, the desire to have that one more thing, or the busyness of life distracts us from focusing on our relationship with God.

Stewardship is a spiritual issue. It's not about what I want but what God wants. I must be willing to submit to the Lordship of Christ.

Rebecca always struggled with an insecurity about money. Not because she and her husband did not have a good income. Justin had a really good job in the computer world, so money was not the issue. It was fear—what if we get in a financial bind.

Justin wanted to start giving a portion of their income to the Lord's work, but Rebecca did not feel the same. She knew they should be giving something, but her insecurities always won out.

Their pastor was teaching a series about trusting God. He said, "Faith is something we are believing for, asking for, or hoping for, without any evidence that it will come to pass." His premise was that it is much easier to trust our abilities to provide than to trust God.

Their pastor encouraged their church family to take a step of faith over the next 90 days and see how God would provide. So Justin and Rebecca felt now was the time for them to start giving. As a step of faith, they began giving a portion of their income to God's work. At the end of the 90 days, they had not missed one penny of the money.

Now three years later, Rebecca finally understands what it means to submit to the Lordship of Christ with their finances. She is reminded of God's protection upon their family during the past three years. Even when their son Tim was spared in a car fire, she was thankful for the Lord protection.

Submitting to the Lordship of Christ involves surrender and sacrifice.

Surrender is to relinquish control to God's plan, while sacrificial living means to put what God wants before what we want. It boils down to the question, what am I willing to surrender to God so he will use me?

Everything we possess, every part of our being, has the potential to be used for God's glory, to advance the Gospel worldwide and to meet the needs of widows and orphans.

Fred and Cindy Fredrick were missionaries to Colombia, South America. Because of God's calling upon their lives they left their home, family, and friends to live in the rural mountains of Colombia. They moved there by faith and lived on a meager salary compared to their friends back in the states. In the early days, they did not even have email, so a letter from home was the high point of their week. They missed their family but with the cost of airfare, they only came home once every two years.

Fred and Cindy did not regret their decision to work in Colombia because they could see God's hand upon their lives. They felt any sacrifice on their part was well worth it because of the lives they saw changed. For more than 20 years they lived in Colombia planting churches and teaching people about Christ. They saw more than 2,000 people make decisions to follow the Lord.

Now they talk about the day when they get to Heaven and how they will meet their brothers and sisters from Colombia. "But godliness with contentment is great gain, for we brought nothing into the world, and we cannot take anything out of the world" (1 Timothy 6:6-7, ESV).

True Happiness

In America, most families live paycheck to paycheck and are burdened with debt, so it is hard to be a blessing to others.

Before World War II most families lived on a single income. Dad was the bread-winner, and Mom ran the house. When the men left home to fight in the war, there was a shortage of workers. With the strong sense of patriotism, many women went to work in the factories to fill the gap in the worker shortage. You may have heard about Rosie the Riveter. During World War II, Rosie the Riveter was a cultural icon representing the American women who worked in factories and shipyards to support the war.[14] After the war many women continued to work outside the home. This change was the starting point of a demographic shift in the workplace.

At first, two incomes meant going out to eat once in awhile or taking a long-dreamed-of vacation. What started out as an *extra blessing* has become a requirement for most families. Now both parents are working because we feel we must. We eat at restaurants four or five times per week and the vacation packages have gotten even bigger. One of the disadvantages of having so much is we continually want more. Even our safety and security are tied up in how much we have. We feel deprived if we don't have everything, so we work harder and put everything on credit cards.

Here is the problem—according to the United States Census Bureau the median household income in 2012 was just over $51,000,[15] and that is in the top 1% of the world for annual income.[16] It's not the amount of money we make; it's the way we handle money and our view of stewardship that changes the way we live.

If we are going to be the hands and feet of Christ, then we need to be willing to submit to the Lordship of Jesus Christ in the way we handle the money God gives us. When we grasp the concept—"It all belongs to God, and I'm the steward" it changes our focus.

The paradox is, the fulfilled life comes not by having more, but by giving of ourselves. God has poured out His abundant blessings upon our country and empowered the church to advance the Gospel worldwide. I believe there are three clear reasons we have been blessed as individuals and as a nation.

> 1) To be a world-changer. Men and women who have a great passion for God do not want to live an ordinary life. Instead, their passion is to change their world and community for Christ.

2) To be a Joyful Giver. God has blessed us so we can give financially to Kingdom causes. Giving is liberating!

3) To be Hands-On. We are truly blessed to be a blessing! God has called each one of us to make a difference where we are.

What will your spiritual footprint be? Each of us will leave a legacy; the question is, what will it look like? How will your influence impact the world for Christ?

It's your legacy - how will you be remembered?

Chapter Six

Giving and Stewardship

What is the first thing you think of when you hear the pastor is teaching a series on stewardship? *Is he going to ask for money?* Or it is time for our annual pledge drive so the church can plan next year's budget? We naturally equate giving as stewardship.

You might be surprised to learn that giving by itself is not stewardship. Please do not misunderstand; giving is something that every believer is commanded to do. But regular giving or even tithing does not mean you are practicing good stewardship.

Where did we go wrong? As a whole, the church hasn't done a good job of teaching stewardship. When you hear a message on stewardship, it is often a segue to, tithes, offerings, and giving. Search the Internet for podcasts, video sermons, or Bible lessons on stewardship and you will see; within a few minutes, they will be talking about giving. Plus, stewardship and giving are topics that most pastors are uncomfortable teaching because we automatically think they are asking for money. That is why the church needs a holistic view of stewardship which includes giving.

A holistic view of stewardship comes from the premise that God is the owner of everything, and we are His caretakers. As His caretakers, we are expected to manage the property God has entrusted to us wisely and see that it grows. Once we have provided for the needs of our family, God wants us to use the increase to extend His Kingdom to every corner of the earth. "When someone has been given much, much will be required in return..." (Luke 12:48, NLT).

Stewardship is simply a matter of the heart and reflects our spiritual walk with God. Plus, it is one of the easiest Christian disciplines to verify. You can quickly see where your heart is by looking at your schedule, your activities, your dreams, and your checkbook.

Giving as a Steward

Giving is a blessing we can enjoy, but it does not happen naturally. A good steward knows it is a responsibility, and a privilege to sow into God's kingdom.

For most people, giving is not easy. We are naturally self-centered, and life gets even more complicated because we have a sinful nature. So the tithe or proportional giving is an indicator of our obedience to God. "Honor the Lord with your wealth and with the firstfruits of all your produce; then your barns will be filled with plenty, and your vats will be bursting with wine" (Proverbs 3:9-10, ESV).

Giving by faith helps break the stronghold of our self-will. The self-will wants to be in control. The self-will is driven by the desires of the fleshly nature we are born with. It pursues its wishes rather than God's plan. Giving takes us towards self-surrender; surrendered to God's influence in our lives. It teaches us to trust God rather than our abilities to make money. It is a sign of submission to God and His Lordship. Jesus told the man, "Take care, and be on your guard against all covetousness, for one's life does not consist in the abundance of his possessions" (Luke 12:15, ESV).

It's not that God needs our money; rather, giving confirms that we have given God control of both the material and spiritual parts of our lives. Each of us will give an account to the Lord for the way we handle the possessions He had entrusted to us. Our goal should be to put God's money to work where He wants us to give. In doing so, we become conduits of God's love so the world will hear the message of Jesus Christ.

Giving also deepens our legacy and the impact of our lives on others. Giving to God's Kingdom work leaves an imprint from our lives on this world for Christ. So give cheerfully, because "God loves a cheerful giver" (2 Corinthians 9:7).

Walking in the circle of blessings is a place we all should desire. First, God blesses you so you can be a blessing to others. When you sow into God's kingdom, Christ is lifted up. You see the fruit of your giving, and that draws you closer to God. He continues to pour out His blessings upon you so that you can continue to give and support God's kingdom work. There's no better place to be than in God's circle of blessings. Giving and receiving, working as God's child to reach our world for Christ.

Kathy Andrews

Kathy is a retired school teacher from Killeen, Texas. About five years ago her church wanted to start an after-school outreach for the children nearby. One problem. They did not have the seed money to start it.

The chairperson asked Kathy if she would be on the leadership team and help get the after school program going. As they developed the plans, organized the curriculum, and applied for the state licensing, Kathy developed a real urgency to see this after school program started. She knew the church was still about $7,000 short of needed funds.

As she prayed, God stirred her heart about giving the $7,000. She knew the only way she could give that amount of money was to take it from her retirement savings. After much prayer and seeking the council of a close friend, she gave the $7,000 needed to start the program.

When the day arrived for school to start, Kathy could hardly wait for the children. She beamed from ear-to-ear knowing God was using her gift to give these children a better chance to succeed in life. Now five years later, Kathy sees how God blessed her so she could help these children.

Kathy's footprint for God will continue to be lived out through the boys and girls in that after school outreach. Those children will get the extra attention they need to thrive in school, but they will also see Christ's love displayed through the school workers. By seeing how your giving is impacting others, it will complete the circle of blessings in your life.

A Generous Heart

Generosity comes from the heart, and it affects every area of our life. The concept of generosity and unselfishness go hand-in-hand. Someone who is unselfish cares for the needs of others even over their needs. Similarly, a generous person is happy to give time, money, or other necessities *unselfishly* for the benefit of someone else.

Giving generously is birthed out of a lifestyle that recognizes God owns everything, and we have been blessed to give. It is not measured by the amount that we give but the attitude in which we give. A generous giver does not look at giving as a burden but a pleasure because they have an eternal perspective. They see giving as an act of worship to our Lord, and their only motivation is to lift up Jesus Christ for all the world to see.

Much has been written about generous giving. In fact, the ministry Generous Giving is devoted to teaching generosity in the Body of Christ. Their website https://generousgiving.org has tools to lead others or deepen your understanding of giving generously.

Several years ago I met Patty. She lived in a small, rugged house in the backwoods of Colorado. In her younger years, she worked in the office of a coal mining company near Trinidad, Colorado. As a widow, she only receives a small pension from her late husband and her Social Security; yet she still gives about 30 percent of her income away. By the world's standards, she does not have very much. Her house needed a new roof, and the carpeting had seen its better days.

On one of my visits I asked her about fixing up her house, but she hated to spend the money on herself when there were so many needs in God's Kingdom work. Patty has a passion to give to God. Based upon the attitude of her heart towards giving she would be described as a generous giver. The dollar amount may be smaller than some, but her passion for God is very strong. Patty believes that God will supply her every need. Patty says her sacrifice is nothing compared to the joy of knowing that people around the world will find Jesus as their Savior.

Sacrifice is a sign of submission and dependence upon our Heavenly Father. When we sacrifice, it demonstrates that our heart is open to God's leadership over our lives. The scriptures declare that it pleases God when His Children sacrifice for His sake. "Do not neglect to do good and to share what you have, for such sacrifices are pleasing to God" (Hebrews 13:16, ESV).

The Jewish people were instructed to bring their best offering (sacrifice), as an act of worship to God. The best animal offering was not the runt of the litter; it was the best available. Even if the best animal could bring a higher price at the market, they would sacrifice their wallet to show their obedience to God.

Most of us do not know what it means to sacrifice. When was the last time you gave up a meal so that someone in another country could have a meal of beans and rice? Or maybe like Patty you decided to wait until next year to replace the carpeting in your house so that you could give to a special project?

Recently I learned how God provided for Patty. During the height oil boom, several investors starting buying property all around Patty's house. She was reluctant to sell, but the price they offered was almost too good to be true. Patty took the cash and purchased a much newer home in town with new carpeting and a brand-new roof! Because of Patty's faithfulness to God in giving, God provided abundantly more than she ever expected.

All of us should give generously, but it requires faith. It all starts with the heart--am I willing to do whatever God asks of me? "For where your treasure is, there your heart will be also" (Matthew 6:21).

I Can't Afford To Give

With our lifestyle many Christians say "I can't afford to give," but I would say, you cannot afford *not* to give.

Some time ago a friend was telling me about their kids moving to a dangerous part of the world on the mission field. His comment was "They are safer in a country like Sudan in the will of God than living in the United States and out of God's will."

Giving is much the same way. You are safer honoring God with your first fruits than keeping the money. Walking with God, in His will, brings protection, security, and peace even in the mist of the storm. Even if you are on the verge of filing bankruptcy you need to start honoring God by giving something.

This attitude is the opposite of what our world thinks. It is a matter of trust. What does God's Word say? ""Will man rob God? Yet you are robbing me. But you say, 'How have we robbed you?' In your tithes and contributions. You are cursed with a curse, for you are robbing me, the whole nation of you. Bring the full tithe into the storehouse, that there may be food in my house. And thereby put me to the test, says the Lord of hosts, if I will not open the windows of heaven for you and pour down for you a blessing until there is no more need" (Malachi 3:8-10, ESV).

We may be hurting ourselves by not honoring God with our giving. According to the USA Today, churchgoers give an average of 2.58[17] percent of their income, and that includes those who give well over a 10 percent tithe.

Could this be a symptom of our out of control spending? What happened to the concept of living on a budget and putting God first? Is our drive for success leaving us void? "One pretends to be rich, yet has nothing…" (Proverbs 13:7, ESV).

In a Barna research study conducted in 2013, 62 percent of Christians said they are just getting by or struggling to make ends meet financially.[18] We feel we can't give because we need to pay off our debt. Unfortunately, we are in bondage because of that debt; "...the borrower is the slave of the lender" (Proverbs 22:7).

Freedom comes with a balanced lifestyle. When we control our spending, we can pay off debt, save for tomorrow and walk in God's abundant blessings by giving today. "Whoever loves pleasure will be a poor man..." (Proverbs 21:17, ESV).

The joy of giving requires *risk*—trusting God. He says, "put me to the test. I will meet your needs."

Teaching your children to give is critical too. Lead them by example and help them learn the joy of giving.

Wise Use Of Giving Dollars

As a steward we are responsible not only to give but to make wise choices where to give. When my in-laws were still alive their mailbox was jammed everyday with appeals from every ministry and organization under the sun. They would ask me, "Where should we give?" "How do we know who to trust?"

My answer was, know the ministry where you are giving. Give to the places where you see God is at work. Know how the funds are being used and what type of return on your investment (ROI) you are getting for your gifts.

The local church is where most people give first. It is the place where we are fed spiritually, have the opportunity to serve, and develop connections for spiritual growth and support.

Many Christians also give outside their local church. Find a place in God's Kingdom work that you are passionate about. Supporting mission projects, working with underprivileged children, feeding the homeless, etc., are all worthy causes but know the ministry that you are giving to.

If you can participate in a community-based ministry, go on one of their outreaches. Help pass out peanut butter sandwiches to the homeless on a Saturday morning, pack food boxes, deliver backpacks, serve food at the mission, or go on a mission trip. See for yourself how they are using your gifts, and discover the passion for Christ of their workers. By seeing how your giving is impacting others, you will see the circle of blessings in action and build your footprint for God.

Think of your giving as a partnership with the ministry you are supporting. The ministry cannot complete their role without the funding, and God has blessed you to give; so it is a partnership. When they share the Gospel, it is as if you are right there with them standing by their side. Few are called to move to Africa, but we can go through partnership. Very few are called to preach like a Billy Graham, D. L. Moody, or Billy Sunday, but you can stand with the great ministries today as God's Word encircles the globe. When you understand your giving in this manner, it will change your whole view on giving.

Look for transparency. We live in a superficial world, and we know very few people deeper than a casual basis. In the day of the mega church and the mega-ministry, it is nearly impossible to see the heart of the leaders. Don't be overtaken by an emotional appeal or a passionate preacher on TV. We've all heard the stories of million dollar homes, fancy worldwide trips, and personal jets. Look for a ministry's openness towards financial accountability, the reliability of their reporting, and their willingness to partner with similar organizations.

Above all, pray for direction. You are accountable to God for the resources entrusted to you. Your giving is your part of the partnership—be a wise steward.

...give, and it will be given to you.

Chapter Seven

Missed Opportunity

Unfortunately, most Christians will miss the opportunity to leave a public testimony of their faith in Christ. By not acting, we make a difficult situation even harder for our family and miss the chance to deepen our footprint for God.

Rosie and Jose were married 37 years when Jose unexpectedly died. Rosie was shocked by Jose's death, but she was devastated even more by the events of the next few weeks. Like most Americans, Jose died without a valid will. Because their house was titled in his name and Jose did not have a will, she lost control of everything and the state laws took control.

She hired a good attorney, but the state said she would only get 50 percent ownership of her house; the kids would get the rest. Rosie felt cheated because she had lived in the house for over 30 years and wrote every single check for all 360 house payments.

What went wrong

Rosie would have been in a completely different situation with some basic estate planning. Unfortunately in all 50 states, without an estate plan, your family loses control, and the government calls the shots. The tragedy is that 60 percent of Americans die without a valid will.

So our spiritual legacy has more to do with creating an estate plan than you might think, and a holistic view of stewardship should include estate planning.

Estate planning is more than wills, trusts, and probate; it is about the people you love. Leaving a properly designed estate plan gives a roadmap to those you leave behind. It's also a great way to share your faith in Christ and provide for the ministries you love too. The simple steps you take today can shape your legacy and your spiritual footprint on this world for Christ.

Time To Be Pro-Active

When someone dies without an adequate estate plan (will, trust, etc.) your state is required to make sure all of their bills are paid and their property is distributed to someone. The technical term for dying without a will is dying *intestate*. In these cases, the state law dictates which blood relatives are to receive your inheritance. The state has their version of a will they use instead of yours, and your family has very little to say in the process. Sometimes this approach backfires and your property gets to unintended people. Take for instance the estranged father who collected one million dollars.

"Kylie was 22 years of age when she died in a tragic accident. Kylie did not have a will and her Estate received a $2M insurance payout due to her accidental death.

Because she had not made a will, Kylie's estate was divided with 50% allocated to each of her parents. This was even though Kylie's father deserted the family when Kylie was six months old[19]."

Stories like this are not uncommon: an ex-spouse who is still the beneficiary on a life insurance policy, an old 401-k goes to an old boyfriend even after marrying another, or the court says your child needs to go live with an aunt that you disliked very much. All of these situations could have been avoided with a basic estate plan.

If you die without a will, a judge gets to decide who will raise your children. Your personal preference and your Christian values may not be considered by the court. Naming a guardian for your minor children in your estate planning documents will avoid this problem.

Also as the parent of a 21 year old college student, you do not have a legal right to close your child's bank account. Without the proper authority expressed in their will, you can do nothing. Even medical care can be problematic. Because of all the HIPPA privacy laws today, a parent may have a hard time getting medical information from the doctor about their child. Several years ago a friend from Tennessee could not turn off their daughter's cellphone after she unexpectedly died because she did not have a will.

By taking steps today to have a valid will, you have the opportunity to provide for your family the way you prefer, plus you can express your love for God and continue your ministry after you are with the Lord.

Why Do We Procrastinate

Death is something we do not like to face. We know it will happen someday but believe that it will be years down the road, so why should I spend the time and money to establish a will today? Here are some of the most common reasons people procrastinate.

I do not have anything. Many people feel they do not have enough property to go through the estate planning process. Owning property is only one of the reasons to have an estate plan. All of the examples from this chapter would have benefited from a thorough review of their estate plan, and most of them did not own property. For a young family, naming a guardian for your children is reason enough to establish an estate plan.

It is too expensive. This is a valid concern for many families, but there are options. Don't let the cost stand in your way leaving your family unprepared or potentially burdened for years. Call several attorneys and explain you are looking for a low-cost estate plan. They might be willing to offer you a lower price or recommend someone in your area who could. You could look for a do-it-yourself kit from an office supply store or an online document service. A note of caution, if you have any concerns about your estate being complicated, because of the people or property, you need to work with a professional. Their expertise will help avoid problems which could end up costing you more in the long run.

Where do I find help? As a Believer, start at your church. Your church office may have some resources to help get you started. Many churches have access to trained people or staff members who can point you in the right direction. Many larger churches have even hired Stewardship Pastors to teach Biblical principles of money management. In addition, some attorneys will provide basic estate planning services at a discounted rate for church members.

It is overwhelming. Getting started is the hard part. Hopefully, you will find it is not as difficult as you expected. The process of identifying your assets and how everything is owned is a healthy experience. You may find a beneficiary that needs to be changed or an old account that needs to be closed. Remember, if your family situation is challenging, you need to find professional help.

Don't put this off any longer. It is important to remember that your estate plan allows you to direct how your estate is handled after your death.

Estate Planning Basics

There are several elements in a good estate plan. Your Last Will and Testament is the most basic estate planning document, but it does not apply to everything you own. Some items like a life insurance policy are considered a contract. As a general rule, life insurance contracts name a beneficiary so they do not pass through your will. Your home is also treated differently and may bypass your will depending on how the ownership is listed on the deed. Each state's laws are different, so it is important to consult with the proper advisors from your area.

In most cases, these are the basic estate planning documents that everyone needs. Your Last Will and Testament is the foundation of your estate plan. In addition, you should have a Living Will, Healthcare Directives, and a Power of Attorney. Estate planning laws also vary from state to state, so they may use slightly different names in your area.

Here is a brief description of each document and what it is designed to accomplish.

> Your Last Will and Testament, is commonly called your *will*. In it, you declare your full legal name along with the county and state of residence. Listed in your will is the person who will be responsible for closing out your estate after you are gone. In addition you will declare who you want to receive your property, along with any special instructions to your family.
>
> A Living Will is different than the Health Care Directives, but in some cases, they are combined. The Living Will is for *end of life decisions*; would you want to be on life support? It may contain a *Do Not Resuscitate* (DNR) clause, or state how you want to be kept alive. Health Care Directives are much broader. They name a person to make medical decisions for you if you cannot express your intentions. It may also include the necessary HIPPA release so your appointed representative can speak to the doctor on your behalf.
>
> The Power of Attorney (POA) for financial decisions designates a person authorized to make financial decisions in your place. The POA can give very broad powers to act on your behalf at any time, or it can give very limited powers for certain situations.

Advanced Tools

Another technique used in estate planning is a Living Trust. A Living Trust is a private arrangement so it avoids the probate court. Living Trusts are powerful tools for those who need in-depth planning, but they are not for everyone. Most people who use a Living Trust want to avoid probate because of the cost; they own real estate in more than one state, or for privacy reasons. Let's look deeper into some of these reasons.

Probate is not bad, but it can be expensive and very time consuming. When you add all the costs, attorney fees, court fees, accounting fees, etc., probating an estate can average about 4 percent of the gross estate. Even an average size estate can cost $5,000 or more very quickly in probate costs. This varies greatly from state to state so check with your local advisors about costs in your area.

Depending on the size of your estate, it may be more cost effective to establish a living trust. In addition if you own real estate in more than one state, a living trust avoids the cost of probate in each state where you own property.

Lastly, a living trust is a private arrangement. In most cases, if your attorney has set up the living trust correctly, you should avoid the probate court, and your records will not become public information.

There are many kinds of trusts that your attorney can set up depending on your needs. They can be great tools if your estate is large enough to benefit.

Practical Steps

There are several ways to keep your most valuable assets out of the probate process. Some of your assets will completely bypass your will. Your accounts with a beneficiary designation and your home (depending on how it is titled) may also bypass your will. Double check your 401-k, and IRA accounts for the correct beneficiary. Take a second look at your life insurance beneficiaries to make sure they are going to the intended people. Also, review the deed of your home to see how the ownership is listed on the title. Joint ownership between spouses may be appropriate in your situation, and that would keep your home out of probate too.

When it comes to assisting your parents, several states allow for a Beneficiary Deed. This solution may be a good move when only one of your parents are still alive. Do not, and I repeat, do not let your parents list your name on the title of their house as a way to avoid probate. This action creates more problems in the long run.

If you plan ahead, you can set up your bank accounts with a Payable-on-death (POD) arrangement. Your brokerage accounts may use a Transfer-on-death (TOD) form of ownership instead. In effect, this allows for a beneficiary to be listed on these accounts too. Every state is different so the names and what they can accomplish may be slightly different in your area. Talk to your professional advisors for what works best in your state.

It may be advisable at some point to discuss your estate plan with your family. It could be an awkward discussion but a necessary discussion especially if there is something unusual about the arrangements. The use of a Minor Trust is a great idea, but if a younger child sees they are not getting all their money until they reach 30 years of age, they might not understand. By explaining this in advance, it will take away some of the surprise and anger. One day they will understand why it is inadvisable to give an 18 year old $50,000 in a lump sum.

A family member may have hurt feelings because someone else received a certain item they wanted. While the boys were both hunters, Jimmy received Pop's favorite hunting gun, and Billy received a handgun. To you, this arrangement may make total sense, but Billy may feel shortchanged. Talking about these situations in advance will help mend those feelings. A hand-written note might be a good way to address these special challenges. Leaving a note with your documents will be a good reminder of why you made each decision.

Marriage Over 50
Second marriages always make planning more difficult, but marriages later in life may have huge financial complications. Retirement benefits, homeowner equity, savings, and investment, plus credit scores all need to be considered when blending a family.

Blended families are very common today, so an estate plan with very specific details is a must. You should double check the beneficiary designations on your life insurance, IRAs and 401k to make sure the right people get the funds you wished them to have. Even if you feel you do not have many assets, you need to take a serious look to make sure every one gets what you intend.

Love is blind is a common saying, but many have been hurt by blind love. You might know someone who has been caught in a situation similar to this.

Becky's brother had been happily married for over 40 years when her sister-in-law died suddenly leaving her brother all alone. Since it was a happy marriage, there was a high probability that Becky's brother would remarry within the first year. Sure enough, that is exactly what happened when Leon proposed to Renee.

The newlyweds settled into their new life and to Leon everything seemed normal. Although Renee did not say anything at first, she felt awkward living in Leon's house. After all, this was the house Leon had lived in for the past 30 years, and his kids were raised in that house too. Leon was a caring man and when Renee wanted new furniture, he was more than willing to buy items to help make it her home too. Over time Leon decided to sell the house so they could buy one together. Depending on what kind of financial planning and estate planning was done when Becky's brother died, Becky's new sister-in-law may have inherited his house leaving his kids out in the cold.

It can be that serious. So why do so many people put it off?

Each day is a gift from God. Don't let life distract you from your most important assignment—love God with all your heart and teach His principles to your family with every footprint of your life.

"So even to old age and gray hairs, O God, do not forsake me, until I proclaim your might to another generation, your power to all those to come" (Psalms 71:18, ESV).

Chapter Eight

Ordinary People

Emma never thought she could leave a financial legacy. In her mind, she was an ordinary person. She knew of rich people who had their name on a building because they gave millions of dollars towards a new dormitory, but she knew that was way out of her league.

Emma is a retired school teacher who never married. She lives in a small one bedroom condo and drives a ten-year-old Chevy. Having lived on one income all her life, she knows how to economize. In her early days of teaching she set-up a payroll deduction account designed for teachers. The agent who helped her open the account almost scolded her, "Never take money out of this account until you retire."

Over the years she paid off her condo, and that payroll deduction account grew to over $400,000. A few months ago when she met with her financial advisor, she named four of her favorite ministries to receive the balance in the account when she goes to be with the Lord. Emma was elated that she could leave a portion of her life, so that others could hear about the grace of God.

Your Christian Influence Can Continue

It might surprise you, but almost everyone can have a financial legacy. You may not think of it as a large legacy, but there are many ways to leave a lasting impact from your life. One area that is often overlooked is giving through an estate plan. It is a great way to leave a lasting legacy for the Lord.

John Winters retired to Sun City, Arizona after working for General Motors for 30 years. The main reason John moved to Arizona was the proximity to Mexico and his mission project in Magdalena, Mexico.

It all started as a young man with his first trip to Mexico in 1975. John went with his pastor, and the mission bug bit him. He fell in love with the kids in the orphanage but especially one of the little girls; Silvia stole his heart. John wanted to adopt her, but because of the legal requirements he was not able.

John continued to support Silvia while she was growing up in the orphanage. Silvia's life was totally changed because of the care she received. She had food, medical care and the education she needed to thrive. The local church connected with the orphanage had a great influence in her life spiritually. It was there she found Christ as her Lord and Savior.

A few years ago John's church had a special speaker. The guest preacher asked the question, "Does your work for God have to stop after your death?" John had never thought about his death this way. He pondered that thought and spoke to his pastor.

His pastor told him with a good estate plan he could continue to send money to support the orphanage for many years to come. That news pleased John to know the orphanage in Mexico will live on because of his giving.

John looks back and sees God's hand in this entire process. He is pleased because his testimony will not stop at his death. His prayer is that people will see his consistent lifestyle for Christ, know how he loved his church, and understand his passion for the work in Mexico.

There are many tools to accomplish John's desire for supporting the orphanage. Finding the right tool is not the hard part. Finding those with a heart to transform the world is by far a greater challenge.

Giving, Part Of Life

Many Christians have considered giving a way of life. Desiree remembered her grandmother teaching her, as a young child, how to give.

Each Saturday she would walk next door to Granny's house to get her allowance. Desiree kept a small glass piggy bank at Granny's because each week Granny would pay her in dimes. Desiree would put one dime in a church giving envelope and the other nine in her piggy bank. That weekly exercise embedded the concept of giving in Desiree's life.

Like Desiree, many of you have been giving to the Lord's work all of your life. So why not continue that tradition and give a portion of your remaining estate to God's work? It is a great way to teach your children about giving by your example. Plus legacy giving is one of the easiest ways to give, and it keeps your options open in case of an emergency.

God wants us to plan for those unexpected medical expenses in life. Plus, with all the uncertainty in the world, we need to protect our savings. But once we pass from this life and are safely in the arms of our Savior, we will no longer need the 401-k, certificates of deposits (CDs), or the nest egg. As you plan for the distribution of your life savings, why not include your church and favorite ministries?

Why Have We Missed Legacy Giving

The church as a whole is not teaching legacy planning as a part of stewardship. In 2013 LifeWay Research released a study showing 86 percent of Southern Baptist churches did not provide any training on estate planning or legacy planning. In those same churches (in 2011), 84 percent said they did not receive any estate gifts either.[20] If we have not taught the importance of leaving a financial legacy, why would the ordinary Christian take this action?

Another reason we might not see much legacy giving is the church has taught us to give from our current income, the tithe. I believe we should be giving at least 10 percent of our income, but what about the assets (houses, land, stocks & bonds, etc.) we call our own? We aren't taught about how to give tithe on the physical assets that we have accumulated or how we should handle giving on the increased value of those assets.

Also, because we have not taken the lead and trained people, we find those who have planned have taken their cues from secular sources.

Most professionals in the financial world know their trade, but typically do not understand biblical stewardship. Rarely do we hear of a financial professional encouraging someone to give away their property, and a church or ministry may be near the bottom of their list.

If every Christian honored God with his or her estate plan, the Kingdom resources needed to complete the Great Commission would be available in our lifetime. Establishing an ongoing system to keep funding the ministries we love not only helps fulfill the Great Commission but increases the impact of our life. All of this works together to become our footprint for God.

What Will My Children Think?

In most circles, it is assumed that you will divide everything equally between your children and no one else. Is there anything wrong with giving an estate gift to someone outside your immediate family? Would God be honored if you blessed a retired missionary with a small gift from your estate? What a great example of stewardship at work in the heart of God's servant.

If your children are believers and understand your heart for ministry, they will not be surprised, and it will remind them of your walk with God. What greater testament of our life could we display for our children.

If your children are not on the same page with you spiritually, it will take some planning to avoid hurt feelings. Don't let that stop you. It may create an opportunity to share Christ with your children as you share this with them before your death. When they see your passion for Christ, they will begin to understand the reason you are giving a small piece of your estate to God's Kingdom work.

Easy Solutions For Giving

We understand giving during our lifetime, but giving after someone dies may be new to us. Here are six simple solutions almost anyone can use to continue their spiritual influence after their death.

Giving through your will or trust: An estate gift through your will or trust is safe and easy. It is safe because you no longer have need of those assets. It's easy because your personal representative (executor) will handle the distribution of your property. One idea is to tithe (10 percent) on your remaining estate. Some families have decided to increase the percentage equal to one of the children's shares. With four children and one share for ministry, each child would receive 20 percent and the final 20 percent would be given to the ministries you choose. You can be creative if you wish, but it is wise to give a percentage to each person or ministry. Account values can fluctuate. and property values change. Keeping the allocation on a percentage basis will allow for a more equitable distribution.

401k beneficiary: Your 401k (IRA, 403b, etc.) is one of the best gifts to give to a ministry since income tax is owed on 100 percent of the value. During your lifetime you were allowed to save for retirement in a tax-deferred arrangement. It is a great way to save for retirement but at some point, the IRS wants the taxes on that account. A tax-exempt organization can be named as a beneficiary (or partial beneficiary) and receive the funds, *income tax free.* The tax savings alone could be worth 20-30 percent making this gift a win-win for God's kingdom work.

Life Insurance: Life insurance can be an easy gift to give to a ministry. By naming the church or ministry as the beneficiary, 100 percent of the proceeds will go to that organization. With some advanced planning, you can receive an income tax deduction by making the gift irrevocable. Life insurance can also be used to replace the value of a gift given to a ministry. Your financial planner can discuss the many options that are available for you.

Endowment Fund: Establishing an endowment fund with appreciated assets provides income in perpetuity (no ending date) for your intended ministry. In addition, it can be used to avoid the capital gain tax. The income from the endowment fund is provided to your favorite ministry each year keeping your financial legacy alive.

Charitable Gift Annuity: The proceeds of a Charitable Gift Annuity (CGA) are paid to a ministry of your choice at your death. Also, a

CGA pays you an income while you are alive. A CGA is a great option when you have investments that do not produce much income, and you want to bless the ministries that you love. Depending on the age of the donor, a CGA may provide more income today and a tax deduction too.

Establish a Donor Advised Fund: A Donor Advised Fund (DAF) is a great giving tool to simplify your giving while you are alive, but it can be used as a giving tool after your death too. In the DAF you will name a successor (a family member or your personal representative) to take over the account after your death. You can give detailed instructions to your successor how you want the funds distributed and to which ministries. The DAF can continue for years or be paid out all at one time. In many ways the DAF is like having a mini foundation. With adequate funding, your favorite ministry could continue receiving your support for many years.

Each of these ideas with the exception of your will or trust can be established without an attorney and with very little cost. Regardless of the size of your estate everyone can leave some type of financial legacy.

Financial Planning

Through the years I have developed an appreciation for good financial planning. An experienced financial planner, who understands biblical stewardship, can help you coordinate your financial plan and your estate plan, so it accomplishes your desires in retirement and beyond. A planner with the right motives (not just wanting a sale) who understands Kingdom giving will be able to show you the best ways to leave a financial legacy. The ministry, Kingdom Advisors, is a good place to find Christians working in the financial world. A *Certified Kingdom Advisor*® has completed specialized training and meets the standards of integrity, experience, and ethical practices to maintain this designation.

Complex Tools

Your financial planner may suggest something more complex. Some of the more powerful tools include charitable trusts, gifts of appreciated assets, leveraged gifts using life insurance, buy/sell arrangements, etc..

While legal documents are required to utilize most of these concepts they can be great planning tools.

Charitable Trusts: There are many variations of the charitable trust. The most common is the Charitable Remainder Trust. It is a great tool for providing income during retirement and avoiding capital gains tax on appreciated property. At your death, the account balance (remainder) goes to the ministries of your choice creating a financial legacy.

Wealth Replacement Trust: Many people cringe at the thought of life insurance, but life insurance can be a great planning tool. A wealth replacement trust uses the income from a charitable remainder trust to purchase life insurance. The life insurance is paid to the family to replace the items given to the ministry.

These are only two of the more complex planning techniques available. It is wise to coordinate your financial plan with your estate plan. Since tax laws change from time to time, it is wise to review your plan on a regular basis with your advisors.

Make an Eternal Difference

You may be like Emma, the retired school teacher, and think of yourself as an ordinary person. That title, *Ordinary Person,* fits almost all of us, but God uses regular people to accomplish His will. With a quick read of Hebrews 11, we see many ordinary people listed as heroes of the faith.

Others that might be considered ordinary people were the three young Jewish boys, Shadrach, Meshach, and Abednego. When they refused to bow down to the idol, King Nebuchadnezzar had them thrown into the fiery furnace; but God spared them. What about the obscure woman we only know as the Widow at Zarephath. With only a handful of flour and a little oil, God used her to provide for Elijah during a severe famine without depleting her supply of flour and oil. Or the young boy with five barley loaves and two small fish that Jesus used to feed the 5,000.

These were ordinary people willing to let God use them to change their world. So what about you? Have you ever dreamed how God could work through you? That your life could make a difference in this world? In your mind, your legacy gift may only be the size of the five loaves and two small fish. But with God all things are possible; leaving a financial legacy is also possible. In fact, it will be the easiest gift you have ever given. Your legacy gift might make the difference as to why someone accepts Jesus Christ as their Savior.

Every day we take foot-steps
that build our spiritual legacy.

Chapter Nine

Finding God's Plan For My Estate

Brianna looks forward to December for more than one reason. She loves Christmas and all of the lights, but she looks forward to the gift of stock from her grandpa. Brianna's grandparents started a candy company in the early 50's, and it soon became one of the largest in the Southeast. For the past five years, Brianna has received a gift of 250 shares of grandpa's company. The combined value was worth over $50,000. Although Brianna has great intentions, each year she sells the stock because she needs the cash.

This scenario is not uncommon. As the manager of everything God has entrusted to me, how do I apply biblical wisdom about my estate? Proverbs 13 says, "A good man leaves an inheritance to his children's children…." Proverbs also warns, "An inheritance gained hastily in the beginning will not be blessed in the end" (Proverbs 20:21, ESV).

What Does the Bible Say About Inheritance
Passing property from one generation to the next was handled much differently in Bible days because their lifestyle was quite different. Most of the time when the scripture speaks of inheritance it is in a spiritual context. In both the Old Testament and the New Testament the overriding theme is the greatest inheritance we can give our children is a strong spiritual legacy.

Hebrew Culture

For the Jewish people, keeping the family legacy alive was achieved through an inherited birthright. This birthright was a place of honor given to the firstborn son. Rarely was there an exception to this Biblical tradition. The birthright would pass the authority of the father to the next generation. At the father's death, the oldest son became the head of the entire family. This gave the oldest son many privileges, but it also carried the responsibility to care for the family and their livestock and sustain the future of the family.

In biblical times most people lived in an agricultural setting. For those who owned land, it was passed to the younger generation during the lifetime of the father so the children could begin working the land. The oldest son would receive a double portion (Deuteronomy 21:17) of the inheritance so he could provide for his aging parents. In many cases, the daughters did not receive any of the parent's property. The daughter's security came from her husband's side of the family.

The spiritual legacy of the family was also passed down through the firstborn son with a special blessing from the father. According to Easton's Bible Dictionary, the birthright made the firstborn son the priest of the family.[21] This blessing meant the son had been devoted to God and became the spiritual leader of the family. So the birthright and the father's blessing had more to do with the family's spiritual legacy than the financial arrangements.

The symbolism of the firstborn is a great picture of Christ becoming the Firstborn of God—the only Begotten Son of God. When Christ took on flesh as the infant, He became the firstborn of all creation (Colossians 1:15). We became heirs of God as part of our spiritual inheritance and enjoy the birthright privileges as a Child of God. "But you are a chosen race, a royal priesthood, a holy nation, a people for his own possession, that you may proclaim the excellencies of him who called you out of darkness into his marvelous light" (1 Peter 2:9, ESV).

The Family Blessing

Even today many families still practice the act of passing a spiritual blessing to their family. It may be as simple as a daily prayer, quoting a

Scripture verse over your children, or learning how to stand on the authority of God's Word. You may pray a quiet blessing that your family knows nothing about, or you could set a time to stand before the entire family like this example.

Nancy Leigh DeMoss and Leslie Basham host the radio broadcast *Revive our Hearts*. One of their listeners shared a personal experience.[22]

> "At the end of my dad's life when he was in the hospital, the family was gathered around him. He asked to hold his one and only great-granddaughter. When she was placed in his arms, he quoted Numbers 6:24-26, "The LORD bless you and keep you; the LORD make his face shine upon you and be gracious to you; the LORD turn his face toward you and give you peace" (NIV). I was real proud of him for doing that—that his mind was so focused upon the Lord and leaving a legacy."

Those final days with a loved one on this earth can leave vivid memories stamped on our hearts for a long time. The wayward son will never be the same as he experiences the passing of his father from this life to his long awaited heavenly home. The final prayer of a grandma, the tightly gripped hand with a silent look of love quietly reminds us of a lifetime of faithful living for Christ. Our goal should be to keep it alive today while we are still young so it will influence our children in their decisions each day.

Passing on a blessing is one way we build a lasting footprint for God. The testimony of a life well lived for Christ. A spiritual legacy like this is priceless.

Earthly Possessions

Today most of us live in cities and receive regular paychecks to support our family. Since our lifestyles are so different than Bible times, it is hard to find a universal formula in scripture for handling the distribution of our estate. In this case, we should apply biblical wisdom of money management in our decisions as we look for God's plan for our estate.

In a consumer based society, we prepare our children to enter the workforce to earn a living and provide for their family. With our banking and investment system, we can save for retirement and prepare for our golden years usually without the help from our children.

One mentor of mine, Ray Lyne with Lifestyle Giving, always said, "In most family situations today, education is probably the equivalent of the Old Testament inheritance. In today's income economy, when we provide education for our children, we provide the equivalence of the land, *the ability to produce*."[23] Ray's point is, in teaching our children how to produce an income with a good career is equivalent to receiving a plot of ground to farm. Both produce an income during their life to support their family.

Randy Alcorn points out how life has changed since Biblical times in his blog post, *Should We Leave Our Children Inheritances?* He states, "Today in America, however, things are very different. Inheritances are usually windfalls coming to people who live separately from their parents, have their careers, are financially independent, and already have more than they need."[24]

All of this should remind us the greatest inheritance we can give our children should instill the values of good character, strong education, Christian work ethic, and the legacy of following Christ.

What About My Children

The typical estate plan sounds like this: "I have three kids, and they will each get one-third of what is left." Is that always the best answer? What if one of your children becomes your 24 hour a day caregiver? Should the child that closes out your estate get the same as the one who sits on the sidelines? Life can be messy, and that makes our estate planning messy too.

Our one size fits all approach in America may have created the wrong expectations. As parents, we need to ask ourselves some difficult questions about our family. How should I compensate for a child who owes me money? One study found that one-third of people who received an inheritance had negative savings within two years of the event.[25] Will my children do the same and waste the inheritance? These can be very difficult questions to answer but for the long term health of your family, they must be asked.

How Much Should I Leave My Children

Many parents struggle with this question—and we should. Our decisions should help our children and not hinder them by giving them a large sum of cash at the wrong time. So prayer should be the foundation of this process. Also, the knowledge of our children should play a big part in any plan.

Only you can answer the question, how much is enough for me to leave them? As God's steward, He can give you wisdom in those decisions. Do our children really need the money? Is there a better use of those dollars? Could God use you as conduits to meet the need of another family, a retired preacher living on Social Security, a missionary, or an extended family member. Use this opportunity to bless your children and those you care about including the ministries that you love. Find ways to deepen the footprint for God you leave behind and continue to build your spiritual legacy.

Sharing with Your Children

For most believers having a good public testimony is important, but sharing Christ with your family is paramount. The hand written message of a departing parent will leave a lasting impression on your family for years. While it is possible to leave your testimony in the legal document, a hand-written note, left in your file of important papers will be more effective. A note from you will be seen as a love letter from your heart.

If your children have similar faith values, your hand-written note should encourage them in their faith, serve as a reminder of your family's Christian heritage, and it gives you a final opportunity to share a personal prayer for God's blessings upon them. This note will be treasured for a lifetime.

For non-believing children, your message is just as powerful. Take this opportunity to express your love for them and reminisce about a special memory. Use the time to share what Christ means to you and how your life was changed through your relationship with God. It would be appropriate to share your desire to be reunited one day in Heaven. Close your note with a scripture pointing them to Christ or a prayer for their salvation.

The Big Question

How much money will I need? If you ask most seniors about their greatest fears, somewhere near the top of their list will be, "Will I run out of money?" This question is not uncommon because of all the uncertainty we find in life. God expects us to plan for our retirement days much like He expects the squirrels to save acorns for the harsh winter. We have no guarantee for tomorrow, so we trust God as our supplier.

If you have been blessed with more and have a vacation home in the mountains or a winter home in the south, then rejoice. Your main question should be, "Is God pleased with my decisions about money?" As you evaluate your situation, remember we are selfish by nature, so be honest with God and yourself.

A good financial plan will help you identify your income sources, plan for long term medical care and the unexpected emergencies too. A financial plan may identify some accounts as *only in the worse case scenario bucket*—meaning you may never need this money. When this happens, don't sit on the money, put it to work into God's Kingdom.

Invest In Life

If you find savings that you may never use—*start giving during your lifetime*. Enjoy the fruit of your labor while you are young enough to see how God uses your giving. Drill a water well in Africa, fund a Bible training institute for young preachers in Latin America, or broadcast the Gospel into the Middle East for all to hear. Fulfill God's calling in your life through giving today.

Billy was a saver. His childhood memories were scarred when their family lost their home during the Great Depression. He was a baby, but the shock of it left a fear that remains in his life to this day. As a result, Billy had two goals in life, stay out of debt, and save every penny possible. He remembered the day when he could get a good interest rate on his CDs, but those days seemed past. He didn't need the income, so he decided to do something different.

One Saturday Billy was driving in a strange part of town. As he drove down the narrow streets and saw the unkempt buildings, he thought, "I'm glad it's 9:00 in the morning." He saw people huddled-up all over the place. It reminded him of the people standing on the street corner asking for help. This thought stirred Billy, so he made a visit to the local rescue mission.

When Billy arrived, he met Danny, the director of the mission. As Danny took him on a quick tour of the mission, Billy asked, "Why are there so many people here?"

Danny said, "Their stories are all different, but one way or another they lost their homes, so they have no place to live. Most live on the street and fall through the cracks in the government programs."

Billy could see the rescue mission was more prepared to help than he was, so he went to the bank, withdrew one of his CDs, and gave it the rescue mission. Billy said, "God pays a better interest rate than those CDs. It doesn't matter because my gift to the mission is an eternal investment."

While Billy's gift came from money that he might not ever need, many seniors are reluctant to use those *just in case funds* during their lifetime. That is very normal, but why not earmark some of those savings for ministry upon your death? In doing so, you will continue to spread God's Word for years as you build your footprint for God.

Conclusion
Finding God's plan for my estate is a spiritual exercise long before any paperwork begins. We must start with the question, how does God want me to use the resources entrusted to me? Take time to evaluate

your footprint for God. Know how you want people to remember your life.

For years I wondered about the lives I've interacted with in my younger days. When I get to heaven will I meet the wino that I witnessed to in June 1971 on the streets of Escanaba, Michigan? Will the shopkeeper from Jamaica that came to Christ after I gave her a little Gideon New Testament find me in Heaven and thank me for sharing Christ?

I can only imagine how many hugs I'll share in heaven as I see people from my whole life that were influenced because of my work, my giving and my faithfulness to God.

Let us hold fast the confession of our hope without wavering, for he who promised is faithful.

Chapter Ten

Every Footstep Counts

Take one look at our world and you can see the evidence that the end of time is near. Violence in the Middle East, threats of homegrown terror, the decline in social values along with apathy in the church makes us feel hopeless, but we are not without hope. Our footprint for God is more important now than ever. Putting the concepts of this book together and applying them will make our footsteps more effective for Christ.

It's Time

It's time to get serious about walking with Christ. We can impact our world and influence others for eternity. As our culture becomes more secular, we must share our faith deliberately. If Christ doesn't return in our lifetime, we need to prepare our family and those we love for some difficult days ahead.

The evidence is clear. Just over 50 years ago the United States Supreme Court removed prayer from public schools. Since then moral values have constantly declined. Legalized abortion on demand, the breakdown of traditional marriage, the acceptance of assisted suicide, and the government forcing businesses to provide the morning-after pill as part of routine healthcare.

Many of these social changes have become the norm, especially in the past ten years. Imagine where our country will be if our moral values continue to decline at this pace for the next 50 years. Our country could become a godless society. You might wonder how this could happen in a country founded on freedom of religion, but it has happened. In the past 100 years, there has been an assault on Christianity in at least three major countries of the world.

In 1914 there were 84,766 Russian Orthodox churches and chapels in Russia--before Russia's anti-religion campaign began.[26] "Lenin's decree about the separation of church and state in early 1918 deprived the formerly official church of its status of legal person with the right to own property or to teach religion in both state and private schools or to any group of minors."[27]

In China, there were 3,300 missionaries in 1919, before the Chinese government tried to eliminate the Christian church.[28] The Communist Party of China officially organized in 1921 and continued to gain power over the next 20 years.[29] "After the victory of the Chinese Communist armies in 1949 and suppression of religion, the members of all missionary societies departed or were expelled from China."[30]

Even in Germany, there was a mass assault against the church. In January 1933, sixty-seven percent of the population were members of the Protestant Church.[31] "As Hitler grew more powerful, his religious tolerance disappeared, and he tried to replace Christianity with a new Reich Church, a religion in which there was no god but Hitler."[32]

My concern is not a prediction but a wake-up call for the Christian Church. Your example of a Spirit-filled life will show your family how to live for God in what could be a difficult future. This realization alone should cause us to evaluate our walk with Christ and drive us to our knees.

It's Time For Personal Responsibility
Everything about my life should point others to the cross. My personality, character traits, the trustworthiness of my speech, my work ethic, and my reputation should line up with God's Word. Am I perfect? No. But I need to take control of my spiritual growth and not be a hindrance to the spread of the gospel. In our consumer-based church,

it's all about what I like. We hop from church to church looking for the right fit, only to find a reason to change churches again next year.

Our focus is wrong, and it hinders our footprint. Our focus should on reaching others. The church is not in existence to meet my needs or to make me happy. The church is a healing place where the shattered and unsaved come for hope. I should work to see others grow in their faith. Focusing on others is how I build my footprint for God.

It's Time For Personal Renewal

We blame the church and the pastor, and then we complain we don't have time to spend time with the Lord. We fail to take responsibility for our spiritual vitality. Is this any surprise? Our society is always looking for someone else to take the blame. What we are missing is a move of God in our churches like the revival at Asbury College in 1970.

On February 3, 1970, without any planning, the Spirit of God began to work through the hearts of those attending the morning chapel service. "The service, a routine meeting, was scheduled for 50 minutes. Instead, it lasted 185 hours non-stop, 24 hours a day."[33] One by one the students and faculty members found themselves praying, weeping, and singing. They sought out others to whom they had done wrong and asked for forgiveness. God's presence was so real that people didn't want to leave. They were afraid they would miss something wonderful.

Their hearts were changed as people cried out to God in repentance. Many rededicated their lives to Christ. The power of God's Spirit caused people to seek forgiveness and relationships were restored. The revival spirit continued for weeks. By the summer of 1970, the revival had reached more than 130 other colleges. Ultimately, it spread across the United States and into foreign countries.

This revival can be traced back to one student who led a few others to take prayer and obedience to God seriously.[34] Imagine seeing a hunger for God like this in our church today. A time when we could not wait to get back to church. In the old days, we would hear about revival services that lasted for hours and would continue every night for several weeks. Where is that hunger today?

Movements of God like this are not new. The Great Awakening was an evangelical movement that swept Europe and British Colonies in America during the 1700s and 1800s.[35] The First Great Awakening brought a deeper understanding of God. The powerful preaching gave listeners the sense of their deep need of salvation through Jesus Christ. At one point in the United Kingdom over 600,000 people had committed their life to Christ through these powerful moves of God's Holy Spirit.[36] God's Spirit continued to empower individuals in our country for the next 100 years. It changed the culture, and North America became the leader in sending missionaries for the world.

Our personal renewal starts with a clear realization that Christ is not a token Savior, but He needs to be our personal Lord. It's time we become serious about our relationship with Christ and take responsibility for our spiritual renewal.

It's Time For Accountability

It's easy to hide in most churches today. Without a connection to a small group or class, there is little accountability. We can slip in during the singing and slip out as soon as the commitment time starts. We attend our non-judgmental services and enjoy our coffee while tapping our foot to the beat of the music. We enjoy the service, but we are not confronted with the Word of God to the point that brings change. Without accountability will we ever see change.

What is missing is a deeply intimate relationship with Jesus Christ, the refilling of the Holy Spirit, and a commitment to be different from the rest of the world. We could see another Great Awakening, but it will not happen until there is a burning desire in our hearts for God. It's time for churches and Christians to draw a line in the sand and stand for Christ.

Stand Tall

Our footprint for God can make a difference, but it will take a strong Christian witness. It will take men and women who will walk in integrity and be known for their righteous living.

Mr. Lew was an honest and dependable man in the community where I was raised. He owned a small family farm with the usual assortment of cows, pigs, and sheep. Mr. Lew was rather quiet about his faith unless you asked him, but the whole community knew he lived for the Lord.

One summer night fire ravaged through a neighbor's barn. The whole community came out in support and to watch because the fire could be seen for miles. Mr. Lew gathered the neighbors in a circle, and they prayed for God to work through this tragedy and to provide for this family.

Knowing his neighbor had a great need, Mr. Lew rose early the next morning to load his truck with feed and supplies to share with this family. Mr. Lew was a great example of a Christian in word and deed. We need more Christians who are different because of the change that takes place in them after surrendering their life to our Lord.

In our post-Christian world, the media portrays the Bible believing Christian as out-of-step with the rest of the world. That is because our value system is not based on the whim of public opinion but on Scripture. The world will never understand or agree with biblical principles, but if we have an outstanding character and are known for an impeccable lifestyle, people will take notice, and it validates our Christian testimony. A great example of how the body of Christ can change the perception the world has about Christianity is by looking at the fast food industry.

I remember going into a McDonald's restaurant about ten years ago. My cheeseburger was prepared with onions, but I had ordered ketchup only. When I took it back to the counter, the young man looked at me as if I was the problem. The level of service at most fast-food restaurants in those days was horrific.

As Chick-Fil-A continued to expand their footprint with freestanding stores, it affected the rest of the fast-food industry. The training program at Chick-Fil-A teaches the young men and women behind the counter what customer service is all about—putting their best foot forward to represent the company well. It is not uncommon to receive a smile or hear words, "My pleasure Sir" at a Chick-Fil-A. A few years later I was in another McDonald's, and I heard the young man behind the counter use the same saying, "My pleasure Sir."

It's time for the church to put our best foot forward and stand tall for Christ. We can show our society that God's children are different. Christians need to be known as outstanding citizens because we represent Christ. This may not change public opinion about biblical principles, but it will remind people that we are Christ's ambassadors.

As Christians, we have a dual citizenship. Philippians 3:20 tells us, "But our citizenship is in heaven…" We may have citizenship in the United States, Canada, or Europe, but our true citizenship is established in heaven. Our loyalty should be to God's Kingdom. The day may come when we are forced to take a stand against public opinion—so be ready.

In our country's race for progress, integrity has gone by the wayside. Situational ethics—*if it's right for me, then it is ok*--has become the law of the land. High profile leaders tell half-truths and justify their actions based on the need at the moment. Like a photo that has been touched-up by Photo Shop, we have no way to distinguish the real truth of the underlining person. Our countries need godly men and women who are role models to our world.

In the book of Judges, Israel was in a similar situation. Israel had ignored God, and there was no judge over Israel to hold Israel accountable for their sin. Israel had turned to idol worship, murder, worshiping false gods, and did all kinds of evil in the sight of the Lord. The Bible pinpoints the problem. "Everyone did what was right in his own eyes" (Judges 17:6, ESV).

Years of sin and rebellion led to God's judgment upon the Children of Israel, and their kingdom was divided into the North and South. Within a few years the Northern Kingdom was forced into exile, and ultimately the Jews were scattered around the world because of their sin. God does not tolerate sin.

Christians are to be the light in a dark world. The voice of our life should beam Christ's love to mankind. Without Christ there is no hope—yet we have that hope. We should be shining examples of His hope to a lost world.

The church is not dead—but we are facing more difficult times. The media portrays the Christian Church as dwindling, but statistics shows that the number of evangelicals has remained steady from 1972 to 2010.[37] The real truth is that the unengaged are leaving the church in droves, but the true believers are still strong. This statistic tells me we need a vibrant relationship with Christ.

Every Footstep Counts

My spiritual legacy. Our life is but a vapor (James 4:14) that will soon fade from this world, but our footprint will remain. The legacy we build should point others to the hope we have found in Christ. Each of us should live the example of the values you want your children to carry on. Leave a footprint from your life which represents Christ to the world.

Wise Stewardship. As God's steward, teach your family how to live and enjoy life while honoring God with your finances. Manage God's resources with integrity and trustworthiness. Teach your family the joy of giving as early as possible so they can walk in God's abundant blessings.

An Eternal Difference. Begin each day with God. Have an eternal prospective and a desire to change the world for Christ. Make every footstep count, knowing God is using you to lead men and women to Christ.

A Financial Legacy. You can continue your witness for Christ long after you have departed from this life. Our decisions about our estate plan should reflect our Christian values. The goal should be to provide for our family while honoring God with the possessions He has entrusted to us. A legacy gift through your estate plan will enable people to hear of Christ's love for generations to come.

It is easy to be overwhelmed by the thought of getting everything organized, but your footprint for God depends on it. Commit to spiritual integrity and living victoriously in Christ.

Stand tall and let God shine through you.

About the Author

Kenn is a speaker, author, and financial coach. His background is financial planning and estate planning and he holds the designation as a Chartered Financial Consultant ChFC®.

Kenn helps Christians develop a biblical understanding of stewardship and answers the question, "Why has God blessed me?" His passion is helping people build their spiritual legacy and leave their footprint on this earth.

Kenn's executive experience includes serving on the headquarters staff of Faith Comes by Hearing and The Gideons International. He worked as a Financial Advisor with American Express Financial Advisors and as a Vice President in Wealth Management for First Tennessee Bank.

Kenn has been communicating with groups of all sizes for most of his career. His diverse background helps him identify with people from all walks of life.

His travels have taken him to more than twenty countries on five different continents to places such as Burkina Faso (West Africa), Cambodia and India. He says his most rewarding experiences have been working with Christian people from all over the world.

How to Host a My Footprint for God Legacy Weekend

The *My Footprint for God* **Legacy Weekend** is designed to engage Christians with their spiritual legacy, develop a biblical understanding of stewardship, and discover that estate planning is part of good stewardship.

Legacy planning has been long overlooked in the church, and most Christians have failed to protect their family with an adequate estate plan. Most believers equate giving as stewardship. True biblical stewardship is much more than giving, and it encompasses all areas of our life including money and giving.

Facts:

In 2011, 84% of Southern Baptist Churches did not provide legacy training to their membership

60-70% of Americans die without a valid will which gives the government complete control of the family's estate.

Description of possible events:

General Awareness—Sunday Worship or Special Event
Designed to give an overview of biblical stewardship and our role as God's steward. Stress the importance of building our legacy each day with a call to financial accountability and estate planning.

Senior Adults—Recognition Dinner to the Honor Senior Adults
Celebrate the life and legacy of our senior adults with the goal to help them finish strong. Stress the need for legacy planning and estate planning as a part of biblical stewardship.

Young Families—Saturday Workshop
Build a foundation of biblical stewardship and why good money management is important. Young families will learn how to build a godly legacy and show how financial planning and estate planning can protect the needs of the family.

Complex Planning--Special Luncheon
Each church has a small percentage of people with more complex planning needs. Business owners, individuals with complex trusts or those who have accumulated wealth. Having a second opinion on your planning options from a biblical stewardship perspective is a healthy endeavor.

A *My Footprint for God* **Legacy Weekend** is a great way to launch a *My Footprint for God* small group in your church. It is designed to increase the awareness of our Christian legacy within the church, plus teach God's ownership of all as part of biblical stewardship.

Note: Kenn does not provide any legal or financial services and does not sell any products.

To find out more or to schedule an event, contact Kenn Edwards at kenn@footprintforgod.com

Building My Footprint for God

Small Group Study Guide

Building My Footprint for God companion guide is an ideal way to take your group deeper in their walk with God. This six-week study is a spiritual journey discovering our spiritual legacy while deepening our understanding of true biblical stewardship.

The footprint of a life well lived offers great opportunity for future generations to know Christ, but many Christians fail to connect the dots. Each decision I make today has an impact on eternity. The depth of my walk with God, the way I handle money, and my priorities in life, all influence my children and those around me for Christ.

The six lessons cover these topics: What is so Important about my Legacy? True Happiness, Blessed Beyond Measure, and more.

Each week is divided into five short lessons with a time for personal reflection. Daily topics include the following: Our Spiritual Legacy, Passion for God, Recognizing it's not Mine, and Ordinary People.

We are all creating a legacy. The question is, "What will our legacy be?" It's our turn to leave a legacy so 100 years from now our great-grandchildren will know why we served God. The absolute best gift you can give your family is a living legacy for Christ.

For more information visit FootPrintForGod.com.

(Endnotes)

1	http://www.winstonchurchill.org/resources/speeches/1941-1945-war-leader/never-give-in Sourced April 14, 2015

2	http://www.personalfinancequotes.com/cat/money1 Sourced on March 20, 2015

3	http://www.breakingchristiannews.com/articles/display_art.html?ID=9507 Sourced on March 20, 2015

4	http://www.liverpoolrevival.org.uk/1859.htm Sourced on January 30, 2015

5	http://www.lifeway.com/Article/Who-is-your-spiritual-hero-mentorship-march Sourced on March 30, 2015

6	http://americamagazine.org/issue/5125/signs/pew-study-estimates-global-christians-218-billion Sourced on April 17, 2015

7	http://www.christianpost.com/news/bishop-td-jakes-talks-living-with-purpose-on-oprahs-lifeclass-72954/. Sourced on April 17, 2015

8	http://americamagazine.org/issue/5125/signs/pew-study-estimates-global-christians-218-billion Sourced on April 17, 2015

9	http://www.christianheadlines.com/news/survey-only-half-of-pastors-have-biblical-worldview-1240810.html Sourced on April 26, 2015

10	http://www.christianheadlines.com/news/survey-only-half-of-pastors-have-biblical-worldview-1240810.html Sourced on April 26, 2015

11	God Owns My Business By Dr. R. Stanley Tam

12	http://www.huffingtonpost.com/2013/08/11/how-this-harvard-psycholo_n_3727229.html Sourced May 24, 2015

13	http://en.m.wikipedia.org/wiki/Charles_Studd Sourced May 25, 2015

14	http://en.m.wikipedia.org/wiki/Rosie_the_Riveter Sourced June 3, 2015

15	http://www.statista.com/statistics/200838/median-household-income-in-the-united-states/ Sourced May 24, 2015

16	http://www.globalrichlist.com Sourced June 3, 2015

17	http://usatoday30.usatoday.com/news/religion/2008-05-31-tithing-church_N.htm Sourced August 7, 2015

18	https://www.barna.org/component/content/article/36-homepage-main-promo/606-barna-update-02-19-2013#.VcTOwko8KrU Sourced August 7, 2015

19	http://www.pt.qld.gov.au/wills/stories.html sourced August 30, 2015

20	http://www.lifeway.com/Article/research-estate-planning-untapped-tool-for-sbc-churches sourced September 19, 2015

21	http://www.biblestudytools.com/dictionary/birthright/ sourced January 1, 2016

22	https://www.reviveourhearts.com/radio/revive-our-hearts/the-priestly-blessing-2/ sourced January 1, 2016

23	Lifestyle Giving, Estate Design Memorandum, Section 1.18, Dated January 2, 2013

24	http://www.epm.org/blog/2015/Jan/12/children-inheritances sourced November 13, 2015

25	http://www.marketwatch.com/story/one-in-three-americans-who-get-an-inheritance-blow-it-2015-09-03 sourced January 2, 2016

26	https://en.m.wikipedia.org/wiki/Anti-religious_campaign_during_the_Russian_Civil_War sourced April 4, 2016

27	https://en.m.wikipedia.org/wiki/Persecution_of_Christians_in_the_Soviet_Union sourced April 4, 2016

28	https://en.m.wikipedia.org/wiki/Protestant_missions_in_China_1807–1953 sourced April 4, 2016

29	https://en.wikipedia.org/wiki/Communist_Party_of_China sourced April 8, 2016

30	https://en.m.wikipedia.org/wiki/Protestant_missions_in_China_1807–1953 sourced April 4, 2016

31	https://en.wikipedia.org/wiki/Confessing_Church sourced April 8, 2016

32	http://www.cbn.com/700club/features/churchhistory/godandhitler/ sourced April 8, 2016

33	http://forerunner.com/forerunner/X0585_Asbury_Revival_1970.html sourced April 8, 2016

34	http://www.calltoprayer.org.uk/encourager47.html sourced April 13, 2016

35	https://en.wikipedia.org/wiki/First_Great_Awakening sourced April 8, 2016

36	http://www.liverpoolrevival.org.uk/1859.htm Sourced on January 30, 2015

37	http://www.usatoday.com/story/opinion/2012/10/18/christianity-christians-pew-research/1642315/ sourced April 9, 2016

www.ingramcontent.com/pod-product-compliance
Lightning Source LLC
Chambersburg PA
CBHW071720040426
42446CB00011B/2147